Foolish

Foolish

Tales of Assimilation,
Determination, and Humiliation

Sarah Cooper

DUTTON

DUTTON

An imprint of Penguin Random House LLC
penguinrandomhouse.com

LIBRARY OF CONGRESS CATALOGING-IN-PUBLICATION DATA
has been applied for.

ISBN 9780593473184 (hardcover)
ISBN 9780593473191 (ebook)

Printed in the United States of America

1st Printing

BOOK DESIGN BY SHANNON NICOLE PLUNKETT

For George, Charmaine,
and Rachael

Contents

Contents

PART 3

Humiliation

Foolish

Introduction

So. YOU'VE DECIDED to read my book. Good choice. I'm not surprised. This book is one of the best books ever written, second only to the Bible.

The crazy thing is, you're reading these words right now. I could literally write anything and you'd read it. Bloop bloop bloop. I just made you read nonsense! Think about your belly button. Boom, now you're thinking about your belly button. I could put any thought into your head right now, much like this guy on the train who's telling me to read the Bible.

That's the power of writing. I love the power. I'm drunk on the stuff. But I struggled. That's right, I struggled. Against myself. Against perfectionism. Against the voice that lives in my head and says, "Why are you wasting your time with this foolishness?"

But enough about the voices in my head, I want to hear from the voices inside yours. Why don't we go around the room and have everyone say:

Your name and life story: _____

_____

_____

Your role on the team: _____

How long you've been here: _____

A dream you had recently that reminded you of your childhood: _____
_____

Your favorite ice cream: _____

Who your mother might have been had she not had you:

_____

_____

Your favorite color: _____

Your ATM PIN code: _____

I'll start. I'm Sarah and here's my life story in a bulleted list because women be skimmin:

- I was born in Jamaica.

- I grew up in Rockville, Maryland.

- I wanted to be a singer, then I wanted to be an actress, so naturally I got a degree in economics.

- I hated economics so I got a graduate degree in digital design.

- I worked at a digital ad agency called IQTV, where I was basically Don Draper in *Mad Men*, if he designed annoying Flash pop-up ads for RottenTomatoes.com.

- I worked at Yahoo!, and I'm not as excited about that as the forced exclamation point makes me seem.

- I quit my job to be an actress and eloped with this guy I met in my acting class and then I got divorced after three months and moved back in with my parents.

- I found stand-up comedy (see previous bullet).

- I went broke (again, see previous bullet).

- I worked at Google, specifically Google Docs. I'm writing this in Microsoft Word and I feel like a traitor.

- I wrote an article that went viral called "10 Tricks to Appear Smart in Meetings."

- I left Google to pursue life as a comedian.

- I got married again.

- Oh my god is this still going?

- I wrote a few books.

- I went viral lip-synching Trump during the pandemic. Which isn't a sentence that should exist in the English language.

- My wildest dreams came true.

- I got divorced.

- Again.

- I learned a whole lot.

- I'm writing a book about it.

- It's the book you're reading now.

Whew. We might run out of time for the rest of you.

A lot of people ask me, Sarah, why do you say a lot of people ask you things when no one's asked you anything? And the reason is, it makes me sound cool. It makes me sound like I'm gonna tell you something a lot of people wonder. And this book is filled with things no one wonders. Then again, who am I to say? Maybe you do wonder how I found out I'm Black, why I've always considered myself the bad roommate, or what Guns N' Roses song I use as a metaphor for my life. If so, definitely read on.

Part 1 of the book is about my family and coming to this country and trying to fit in. My very pragmatic parents brought us here from Jamaica because America was the land of opportunity— specifically, the opportunity to own land. My parents are very proper, God-fearing, and loving, and they value the respect of their community.

The penultimate part is about love and looking for love, but really it's about my ho phase, because I knew my family would like that.

And Part 3 is about my capital-H Ho phase, specifically Hollywood, and my quest to be an artist.

What will you learn in this book? Oh my god, you aren't still reading, are you? How embarrassing.

You don't have to read this. Just post a picture of you pretending to read it on Instagram and you're done. Wow, you're still reading. Okay. Well. I got nothing. Oh, the answers to the other questions, right.

Your role on the team: Recovering individual contributor.

How long you've been here: The whole time.

A dream you had recently that reminded you of your childhood: I dreamed I was Brainy Smurf and no one would talk to me.

Your favorite ice cream: Mint chocolate chip, there is no other answer.

Who your mother might have been had she not had you: She would've been sad because she really loves me, but you'll just have to ask her.

Your favorite color: Please see color chapter, "Periwinkle Can Go Fuck Itself: My Life in Colors."

And my ATM PIN code? Well, I've encrypted that in the third letter of the second word of each chapter title. Have fun, hackers!

As for the rest of you, I hope you enjoy my words. Thank you for reading them.

Bloop,
Sarah Cooper
April 2023
Brooklyn, New York

How to Read This Book

THERE ARE TWO WAYS you can read this book.

The first way is you can read a page, then turn the page. Keep doing that until the end. You'll hopefully notice that each part is chronological *within the part. Sort of.*

For those less adventurous in the bedroom, here's a chronological chapter list, but please be warned, most of these chapters contain sex:

Again, this is only somewhat accurate. Enjoy.

PART I

Assimilation

Jamaicans Go to Disneyland, or World, or Whatever

WHEN I WAS NINE, my parents took us on a road trip to go to Disneyland in Orlando, Florida. Or is that Disney World? Whatever. The point is, I have no idea *why* we went on this trip. I consider this mystery to be my own personal rosebud, even though that metaphor makes no sense.

It was August 1987. Seven years after we moved from Runaway Bay, Jamaica, to Rockville, Maryland—two places that are as different as they sound. We set off from Rockville in our moderately sized silver Volvo station wagon. It was a tight squeeze, three kids in the back seat and one in the way back with the cooler and our luggage. It was a real no-man's-land back there with the cooler, so George, Charmaine, Rachael, and I traded off. The four of us lived for fast-food stops. But my dad lived for getting wherever we were going as quickly as possible and using that as a conversation starter whenever we got to wherever we were going.

My father was 44 at the time, which is one year younger than I am now. And I don't have a family of six. I am single and live alone and just got back from Trader Joe's, where I procured some frozen fish sticks for dinner.

"We made good time," my dad would say very seriously to whomever. "I calculated three hours but it only took two hours and fifty-eight minutes." A sort of Harry Belafonte meets Bill Nye the Science Guy, my dad was well into his 17-year career as a safety engineer for the Washington Metro. On this trip he was relying on a state-of-the-art navigation system called My Mom and a Paper Map. My mom's 37-year-old eyes were glued to the road. Along with being the navigation system, she was second-in-command and keeper of the peace.

George was 17 and would be off to the Navy soon. And he was very skinny. And very cool. He'd say things like GOOOOOOD NIGHT! Like that guy did on *Good Times*. I always wanted to impress my brother. He'd give me a high five and it would hurt so bad but I'd pretend it didn't. This created a real fear of high fives in me that lives on to this day. Charmaine was 15. Rachael was 11. And I was 9. You could say we were a handful but we were never loud, because Daddy needed to concentrate. We did NOT want to miss an exit. There would be nothing worse than missing an exit. If that happened, my dad would lose his temper and curse up a storm. The car would get anxious and quiet. But as soon as the problem was solved, he was whistling again. I'd still feel anxious for a while, though, even as he whistled. I think that's why I hate whistling.

Here's a secret: My dad is the reason I have no idea why we went on this trip. He wasn't a fan of fun or leisure in general. If we were watching TV, he didn't sit down and watch it with us. He'd stand in the doorway, with his arms folded, until something silly happened, then he'd say we were watching rubbish and walk away. To this day I feel bad that my dad doesn't know how so many movies ended. He has no idea that Aladdin winds up with the princess or that Mary Poppins leaves the family. He doesn't even know who those people are, nor does he care!

My dad was always pretty stressed out, and I don't blame him one bit. I'm 45 years old and had to ditch my fish stick dinner because I just found out I can't cook them in the microwave and getting out my frying pan feels too daunting.

Sometimes I try to put myself in my parents' shoes. And I think if I were them, I would never have taken us on that trip. As I write this, I have no family, no responsibilities, and I'm about to micro-wave some chicken nuggets for dinner.

A few months ago, I asked my mom why they took us to the DL. And she responded with just one word: "Marriott."

"Marriott?" I said.

"Marriott," she said.

I implored her to elaborate. And she did.

"Since I was working at Marriott, we could get a special rate at Marriott and save some money at Marriott." (This chapter is not officially sponsored by Marriott, but I'm open to taking calls.)

This still didn't make any sense to me. If they wanted to save money, wouldn't we have just stayed home? I do have a degree in economics.

My family didn't go on vacations. We only went to Jamaica. Ugh, Jamaica. My friends were all so jealous I was going to Jamaica. Little did they know, it was the most boring place on earth. All we did was see family. And it felt like we were related to everyone. I was constantly being introduced to people—*This is your father's cousin! This is your Aunt Josie from Kingston on your mother's side! This is your mother's father's cousin's son's uncle!* And I'd just go, okay great! And give them a hug. The adults spent all day talking and talking and talking and all we were allowed to do was keep quiet and wait. (Just to be clear, I love my family and I love Jamaica, in fact, I just spent 10 days there and I will be going back very soon. But as a child, it was mind-numbing.)

My dad also drove us everywhere when we visited Jamaica. But I-95 was a picnic compared to him on a one-way Jamaican back road, with a steep cliff down to the ocean on your left side, and on the right side, oncoming traffic because, oh yeah, we're driving on the left side. In the rain. With cars passing. While trying to avoid people and dogs and chickens and goats. These trips are the reason I've still never seen any film in the Fast & Furious franchise. In America, I'd see those commercials with "One Love" playing, telling you to come to Jamaica, and I'd be like, yeah right, no thank you!

Jamaica might be my homeland, I mean, it is my homeland, but it was on that trip to Disneyland, or World, or whatever, that I discovered my home: hotels. I fell in love with fancy lobbies and continental breakfasts and tiny versions of things in buffets. Tiny little ketchup bottles. Tiny little raspberry jam jars. Tiny little individually packaged tabs of butter. I marveled at these individually wrapped tabs of butter, with their convenient vacuum seals and peel-off technology. And it was all free! I loved the rooms—how everything was neat and orderly and minimalistic. I didn't even mind that you couldn't open the windows. Give me the cool, recycled air of a hermetically sealed bedroom any day.

And, of course, there were the pools. Charmaine, Rachael, and I would spend hours in the hotel pool and imagine we were synchronized swimmers and make up routines. I'd pretend I was a mermaid and wiggle through the water like Daryl Hannah in *Splash*. Remember when she leaned back in that white bathtub, her fin unfurling in front of her? That was going to be me someday, I just knew it. We were jumping into the water and screaming and splashing like nothing else mattered because we were on vacation.

When we finally got to Orlando, my favorite part was, of course, the Marriott. It had a glass elevator. I'd never seen one before. It rose several stories above the hotel itself. We rode it all the way to the top and we could see all of Disneyland or World or whatever.

The park was fine, but I thought the It's a Small World ride was too slow and all I really remember is walking a lot and trying to take pictures with all the different characters even though I didn't know who most of them were. And then it was time to go home. Or so I thought.

The trip wasn't quite done. Before we left Orlando, we went to visit my half sister, Ann-Marie, who was a few years older than George and lived there with her mom. I didn't fully understand how I was related to her, and I thought, *Oh no, not more family, that's only supposed to happen in Jamaica!* But she was lovely and so sweet and I gave her a big hug and wondered if this whole trip was a ruse to visit Ann-Marie.

On the way home, we stopped in Fort Lauderdale. For those following along on your paper maps, you're right, Fort Lauderdale was four hours out of our way. Why would a man who lived and breathed efficiency do this? Well, the answer, my friends, is blowing in the wind, specifically the hurricane we had to drive through to look at some land my dad had purchased while he was still in Jamaica. He was very excited to see this land, but it turned out to be a marsh. It was very wet. Dad was like, "Look, this is our land!" And I was like, "Cool. When are we going to the Marriott?" After checking out of the Fort Lauderdale Marriott, we were finally on our way home.

So why did we go on that trip? Well, my guess is it was all of the above. Because if there's one thing Jamaicans know how to do, it's kill two birds with one stone. And I'm so grateful for this gift my parents gave us. It must've been pretty stressful for them. Or maybe I'm projecting, because these chicken nuggets are not great and I might have to order tacos.

Because I'm the Washbelly

I AM THE WASHBELLY. I was born a washbelly, and I will die a washbelly.

"Washbelly" is what Jamaicans call the youngest child, the person who "washed out" their mother's belly. Washbellies are known for being lazy and spoiled, which seems mean but is accurate.

I hate the name washbelly. To me, it sounds really gross. But, despite the distasteful moniker, I own my washbellyness. I love being the washbelly. I love that no one expects anything of me. It only sucks when you get older, and people start expecting things of you.

Growing up as the washbelly, every day felt like the first day on the job. I didn't need to bring anything to the table. I'd just show up, and stuff would already be there. Someone else always had the information, someone else was always in charge. Now people look at me like I have the information and I'm in charge, but I don't have the information and I'm not in charge. Because I'm the washbelly.

That's why I love a new audience. I hope you aren't reading this for the second time. Don't get to know me too well, you'll only be disappointed.

How did I become the washbelly? Glad you asked. Best segue ever.

It was 1967 in Mandeville, Jamaica, and everywhere else in the world, too, probably. Jennifer was 17. Gorgeous. Like a Jamaican Brigitte Bardot. She made all her own clothes and always looked stylish. Miniskirts, minidresses, tight pants, polka dots, name a fun 1960s fashion item, and she was in it.

My father, Lance, was 24. A smooth cat who, according to him, had seven or eight girlfriends at the time.

That summer, Jennifer got a job as a bank teller. It was the same bank where Lance went to deposit his checks. And when Lance saw Jennifer, he didn't think twice before scooting over to her line. And he wasn't the only one. Jennifer's line was always the longest. But Lance didn't give up. He'd wink at her, show up when she was leaving and offer her a ride home. He was trying to be cute and flirt, but Jennifer thought he was trying to rob the bank! Soon she was scared to show up for work. She wondered if she'd become an accomplice. It was all very romantic.

Some weeks later, Lance told Jennifer he wasn't trying to rob the bank, he was just really into her. Jennifer decided to give him a chance. Jennifer's mom always told her that it's more important for the man to really like you than for you to really like him, a maxim she repeated to me, and one I truly believed right up until my second divorce. In those days, if you were a woman and you weren't married by age 20, you were an old maid, and so my mom knew time was running out.

On their first date, my parents-to-be drove to Montego Bay to watch the planes take off. I like to think they were already daydreaming about flying away. From day one, my dad was calling my mom his wifey. My mom told him to stop doing that because people would get the wrong idea. But in two years, she did become his wifey. They were married in September 1969. And like all marriages, theirs was filled with joy and hardship and surprising silver linings.

Several moons later, my brother, George, was born.

When George was six or seven, he was in a drowning accident. I did mention the hardships, right? He was in a coma for several weeks and they thought he was going to die. But he was nursed back to health and miraculously made a full recovery. And today, he doesn't remember any of it. In fact, he didn't even know he'd been in an accident until he was 17 and told my mom he was joining the Navy. She freaked out because she knew he wasn't so good with bodies of water. When she told my brother about the accident, he shrugged and joined the Navy anyway.

A few years after George, Charmaine was born. She came into this world deaf and had underdeveloped bones in her face, a very rare congenital birth defect called Treacher Collins syndrome. Like I said: hardships. The doctors told my mom she would probably only live three months. But she's a fighter, and Mom and Dad did everything they could to give her a happy, healthy life. They flew from Jamaica to London to get her the surgery she needed to be able to hear. She's 51 now and a very successful nurse practitioner, a path she was inspired to take by a nurse who was kind to her when she was in and out of hospitals as a kid.

Four years after Charmaine came Rachael, and a year and a half after Rachael came me. The washbelly. Sarah Cooper. I'm the one writing this book.

I was due on Christmas, but my mom wanted to be home on Christmas, so they induced labor. I've been punctual ever since. My dad says I was already holding my head up after I was born because I was so excited to see him. I don't remember, so I just have to take his word for it. When my mom saw I was healthy, she asked the doctor to tie her tubes and she was done making babies. And that's how I became the washbelly.

When Mom was pregnant with me, Charmaine thought she was going to get another brother because as mom's belly grew, everything she sewed was blue. When I came home from the hospital, she remembered that I was always giggling. Charmaine wanted to see if I looked like her and was a little disappointed when I didn't, but she loved playing mom and would take me and Rachael out for a stroll to the market down the street. After Charmaine had surgery and was able to hear music, she would dance, and I was her audience.

Since we were only a year and a half apart, everyone thought Rachael and I were twins. Probably because Mom sewed matching outfits for us and told everyone we were twins. Rachael was always a year ahead of me in school, until one day she and I were in the same class! I was so excited. But she wasn't there long before they removed her to put her in special education, and I missed her so much. I mean, she laughed at all my jokes. Even when I was trying out new material. And she was always very generous. She never held back. To this day, if something is really funny, she'll laugh until there are tears rolling down her face and she can't breathe. That's the laugh I'm always going for.

WHEN I WAS ABOUT A YEAR OLD, my mother left Jamaica for three months, in case you want to know where all my abandonment issues come from. As codependency legend has it, every day I would sit outside on the steps waiting for her. When she finally came back, she says I wouldn't even look at her. That's right, the silent treatment. The cold shoulder. But soon enough, I was back in her arms. And then she left again. And then she came back. Cold shoulder. Back in her arms. Now you know the complete trajectory of all my relationships in my twenties.

I found out pretty recently that the reason my mom kept disappearing is that she was location scouting our new home in America. She wanted to leave Jamaica because crime was rampant, and she wanted a change.

My dad didn't want to leave. To him, moving to America was too risky. One wrong move, and we'd be homeless, he told my mom. One mistake and it would all be over. My father is a chill dude. But things were tough for him growing up. He was an only child being raised by his grandmother in the rural village of Green Valley, Jamaica, and he literally had to walk three miles to get to school. Being poor, he vowed to himself that, with God's help, he would work as hard as it took to be successful. And he did. My dad graduated from college at age 20 and started work as an electrical engineer at the Jamaica Public Service Company and then the Kaiser Bauxite Company. For my dad the only achievement is overachievement.

My mom grew up in the parish of Saint Elizabeth, with her father, mother, and 10 siblings. That's right, I said 10. My grandmother, or "Mama" as we called her, had seven girls and three boys. My mom was very close to her sisters, but one by one, they got married and moved away. And one of my mom's sisters, my aunt Polly, had just moved to Rockville, Maryland, outside Washington, DC. And when I was three years old, Aunt Polly and Mom finally convinced Dad to move to Rockville, too.

Dad started his career at the Washington Metro. Mom got a job as a secretary. Dad was soon head of his department. Mom was soon head of HR. And together, they gave this Jamaican family a big old slice of the Middle-Class American Dream Pie.

We commemorated our new lives as all Americans do: with a family portrait at JCPenney.

That's me down front. Because I'm the washbelly.

Diary: The Gulf War
and the Poison Concert

THE FOLLOWING ARE DIARY ENTRIES from the journal I kept when I was 13. They are written in the most exquisite cursive, except when I got lazy. Spelling and grammatical mistakes left for full effect.

Thursday, January 10, 1991

Dear Diary,

This week has been very easy. It hasn't been great but it wasn't all that bad either. Monday we got off of school because of 6 inches of snow! Tuesday was easy. I showed everyone the pictures of the kids I took. Benjie was embarrassed that I took so many pictures of him. That day I didn't talk to him much at all. Tuesday night it didn't snow but the roads were covered with a sheet of very slippery ice. So we got off that day, also. Sean called me. One of his friends, named Chadeus (I can call him Chad) was on the other line. We spoke for a little while and then he hung up. He wants me to "get with him" on Saturday night. But I just quaintly refused. I don't want to be tied up with him. (Mentally that is, not physically) Today was an okay day. This morning on the bus we (all the kids) were talking about the Gulf Crisis and Saddam Hussein. You see, there is going to be a war, supposedly on the 15th between

Saudi Arabia and the US. We are fighting over this very small city called Kuwait because Kuwait has a lot of oil. My brother is going there this year. I was very upset on the bus this morning. I mean my sisters are close to me but not as close as George is. Anyway, Benjie and I talked a lot today. We smiled and laughed with each other. I went to Blair tonight for an orientation meeting. It seems like a real nice high school. Well David and Kelly are getting closer now. They make a very nice couple. I was watching them talk together on the bus today. I can tell that they like each other a lot. I'm not jealous of Kelly. I'm just jealous of their relationship.

Love,
Sarah

Wednesday, January 16, 1991

Dear Diary,

Well, no TV sitcoms tonight. It's all news. Yesterday, the 15th, was the deadline for Iraq to with draw from Kuwait and today, at sometime between 5 and 6 p.m., war started. Bush made a speech which was really good. They say that there is almost no doubt that the US will win. I spoke to George today. He's not worried at all. He may not be going but maybe he will. I sure don't want him to. They keep playing this song on the radio called "Show me the way" by the Sticks. It's pretty sad. Tomorrow everyone is going to where yellow to show our support for the troops. My mom has been watching the news forever. I mean, it's 12:32 and she's still watching. Oh well, she's just worried about it. Worrying too much if you ask me. What to be will be, you know? Anyway enough about the sad present. Let's talk about the past. Saturday night I slept over Lena's house. We got up at 4:30, actually I never slept. We went to

Hecht's and only one other person was there. Oh, if you're wondering—we came to get tickets for the Poison-Trixter concert. We got 15th row tickets at 10:00 in the morning. I called Sean. We talked to Yule, who I am not getting along with. Maybe it's because of the poem I wrote to Sean. (Sean was speechless.) So that night Stace and I went to the rink. Kate waz there with her popular friends. Stacey says she was real mad at Kate but then she turns around and is her friend again. Stacey won't admit it but I know she wants to be in with that group. It's fine with me, just as long as she doesn't leave me in the dust. Monday waz boring. I went to Richard Montgomery for orientation and I really like that school. I have a better chance there than at Blair. Tuesday I skipped school. Wednesday, well, today we went to career fair. Monica let me put on some eye liner. After that everyone was saying that I looked good. (I can't wear it, though, mom!) Danny K. and Chris R. made B-ball, so did this guy Rashad. Black. <u>NICE</u> body. Muscular arms, strong chest. Really hot. I sat near Benjie today at lunch. We had a GREAT time. Lena and I are close now. She's having a HUGE party this Saturday. (Rashad and Brook coming) Everyone's coming! (PS—Brook looked REALLY good today. He sat next to Wendy the whole lunch though)

Love,
Sarah

Sunday, February 17, 1991

Dear Diary,

I have so much to tell you. The reason I haven't written in a month is because I couldn't find you. I just KNOW Charmaine took you. But, oh well. Let me start at the beginning. At Lena's party, well I got there pretty late. The night before I spent at Stace's house. There was a White Oak Dance that night and Adam was going with this 6th grader named Brooke so I didn't see him. We had a pretty good time. And so I got there at about 9:00. People were hanging out at the porch they all said Hi to me. Brook, who was going out with Wendy at the time was making out with Wendy on the couch the whole night. Terry put his arm around me once (and Kelly). Ashley and Danny M. made out on the ground outside. All the guys were mooning the camera. I can't wait until those pictures come out. I really had a good time. That week Wendy and Brook broke up, um the next week Kelly fell in love with him and they went out and I think it was that week that Adam called me and wanted to "talk." Well, at the time I was in awe of him calling me. His little 6th grade girlfriend was the main subject though. He said he was gonna break up with her. He got dumped the next week and called me again on Friday and Saturday. By then I had heard that he liked Sarah Eisen. He told me that he liked me. Now I'm not jealous. I was and still am going out with Sean right now, not happily, but I am. I saw him at a game. He looked so bad. I'm sorry but he did. So this is the first weekend he hasn't called. Anyway Brook broke up with Kelly after 4 days.

Now this has been the most AWESOME WEEKEND I have ever had. Last night was the concert of the season of the year and of my entire life POISON! TRIXTER! It was awesome. Let me start at the beginning. I went over to Lena's at 2:00. Megan (oh Megan is the other girl that went, she's a real good friend of mine now). We got dressed many times. I had no idea what to wear. I ended up wearing some tights, jean shorts and a shirt.

We left at about 5:10. We went to KFC and got chicken. We got there and there were a million cute guys there. We went in. Trixter played first. They were great and they looked, sounded and acted exactly the way they do on their videos. "give it to me good" was their best song which they sung last. Everyone was standing up

and clapping and putting their hands like this [author note: here, I drew a picture of an "I love you" hand sign] *or one's or fists. Then there was intermission. I bought a tour book for 13 dollars. Lena got 2 t-shirts and a underwear. We went back and POISON came on! They all looked exactly like the pictures, but better. Rikki Rocket did a drum solo and the drum said "Fuck Iraq." Right before Bret Michaels sang "Something to Believe In" he said "if we want peace we shouldn't be over there but while we are we might as well fucking kick their asses!" and everyone screamed. C. C. Deville did a guitar solo that must have been 15 minutes long and Bret did a harmonica solo which was sort of bluesy and everyone was clapping the best part was at the end when they turned the lights on and Bret came back out. I went up to the stage and I was 5 feet from his face. I was in awe. I should've said something but I couldn't talk. A guy from the crew came out and gave out the picks that Bobby Dall played with. I just had a feeling that I was gonna get it. I looked down and there it was! It's green and it says Poison on the front and Mr. Dall on the back. Oh, it was the best concert ever! And this is the best weekend ever! Bye!*

Love, Sarah Loves POISON

Black Enough to Be Called It, Not Black Enough to Say It

WHAT ARE YOU? That's a question you don't get every day. Unless you're me, in which case you get that question a lot. I get that question from everyone. Including myself, after I've eaten too much bread. And the answer to that question, in both cases, is I don't know.

Maybe I should find out. Maybe this chapter should be a deep dive into my ethnographic history, like a reality show about my ancestors sponsored by 23andMe, most likely now owned by Amazon. Or perhaps this chapter should be a full-throated rejection of our relentless desire to categorize and codify every person we meet. Then again, maybe it should just be jokes about the N-word. The point is, this chapter could be anything. And so could I.

I've never really felt Jamaican. Especially because my parents keep telling me I'm not Jamaican, usually when I refuse to eat oxtail or ackee and saltfish. Growing up, I never thought about race. Maybe I thought I was white. But one day I found out I was definitely not white. This is my coming-out story.

It was a spring day, sometime in the late 1980s, and I was walking home from the bus stop with my best friend, Stacey, who was Jewish (she still is).

Stacey and I always came home from school together. After we got off the bus, we'd walk home, drop off our stuff, and meet in the street to play. Our neighborhood was a new development, everyone there was the first person to live in their home and some homes were still being built, and we'd explore around the construction sites. We'd walk down to the creek and catch tadpoles. We'd run around until dark. Then we'd go over to her house, make up dances, prank call florist shops, and complain about our hair (I wished mine was like hers and she wished hers was like mine). We had so much freedom.

We were both very entrepreneurial and every summer we had a moneymaking scheme. Cat sitting, dog sitting, plant watering. Grown adults would literally hand us the keys to their homes for weeks on end and I'd tell my parents I was going to go water plants or feed a cat and then I'd just go hang out with Stacey at some random family's house, peek through their bookshelves, order Domino's, watch TV, and even get paid a handsome $10 for it.

Anyway, on this particular day, we were walking home from the bus stop and out of nowhere, Stacey tells me that an older kid called her a "n****r lover." I was like, why would they call you that? And she said, because my best friend is Black. And I was like, wait, I thought I was your best friend? And she said, you are. And I was very relieved that Stacey did not have a secret best friend, but also very confused as to what made her a "n****r lover." And she said, because you're Black. And I was like . . . I'm what?

And I ran home and I said, *Mama, Papa, I think I'm Black!* And they said, *No mon, we're Jamaican!* And I was like, *Wait . . . I think you're Black, too. I think our whole family is Black!*

At the time, we were learning about the civil rights movement in class. We'd just watched a video of a bus of African Americans being set on fire, and all of a sudden, I wondered if that was going to happen to us, because I was young and I made everything about me and I definitely don't do that anymore. Would I be hosed down at a diner counter? Was my dad going to be shot? My only knowledge of Blackness was slavery and Jim Crow and racism. Once, when I was hanging out with Stacey, our other friend, a white girl named Kate, spit in my face. She apologized and said it was just something she saw on TV. I asked my parents if all white people were bad. They said thinking all people are one thing just because of their race was the root of the problem, and I shouldn't think that way. I hope Kate's parents told her something similar.

I'm not sure I would even be asking these questions about what I am had I not been *getting* these questions. No one asked me questions like these in Jamaica. Not to brag, but Jamaica is a politically independent majority Black country. Not to brag harder, but Martin Luther King Jr. said in Jamaica he felt "like a human being." And I did not just find those two things out when I was writing this chapter.

Anyway, I was pretty sure I was Black. But my parents said we were Jamaican. And I was keen to figure out the difference. But whenever I asked my parents what my ethnicity was, I always got a different response. *Well, you know your great-grandfather was Chinese. Your great-great-grandmother was Indian. You have Dutch and Irish in you, maybe German, too, who knows!* And then they'd recite the national motto of Jamaica: *Out of Many, One People.* This was their answer for everything. Then they'd start naming famous people we're related to. *Heavy D is your cousin. Colin Powell is your cousin.* Pretty much if they were a famous person with Jamaican heritage, they were my cousin. I was like, okay, so I'm all races and related to all Jamaicans. Thanks, Mom and Dad, that really cleared things up. Glad I didn't pay for these results.

A few years ago, my then-husband wanted to do 23andMe. And I figured my DNA result would just be the shrug emoji in every skin tone. But I did it anyway and I found out I am 1 percent Ashkenazi Jew! Did you know there were Jewish people in Jamaica? Jamaican Jews! I feel like my whole personality makes so much sense now. But something I wasn't expecting was that nowhere in my result did it say Chinese. And I know my dad's mom was at least half Chinese. What does that mean? Maybe my dad isn't my dad?

Or more likely, 23andMe is a scam. They're mixing up samples. The data is fake. And I'm not just saying that because I have stock in Ancestry, now owned by Blackstone.[*]

Making It in America™ seemed like it was all about being as white as possible. White skin, white teeth, white sales. Every few years we'd move into a bigger house and a whiter neighborhood, until there I was, the only Black girl in AP History.

Unsurprisingly, my college boyfriend was a white dude named John. And I once asked him if he wished I was white. John laughed and said of course he didn't. And then he asked me if I wished I was white. And I was like . . . sometimes?

But I don't wish I was white. Can you imagine how white I would be if I was also *actually white*? I am proud to be Black, I just wish people knew I was Black, or at least accepted it when I told them.

At Google, my manager IM'd me once and said, "Sarah, I'm doing the diversity report, is it okay if I say that you're Black?" And I said, "I am Black." And he goes, "Oh great, even better!"

Black women are not a monolith, but even in the vast spectrum of Blackness I don't know where I am. Sometimes, I can't tell if I'm a Black woman or a white dude named Craig.

For example:

- I worked at Google.

- At least once a week I think about starting a podcast.

- I had a Jamaican nanny growing up (she was family, her name was Marva).

- I've been asked to stop saying the N-word.

- I've been asked to stop saying the phrase "the N-word."

---

[*] Not really. Though, again, happy to take calls.

- There are certain words I can't say, like "stuntin."
  Or "deadass."

- There are certain words I keep trying to say, like "stuntin"
  and "deadass."

- I have never been to WorldStarHipHop.com

- I believe I'm a member of Black Twitter but I don't know
  how to check.

- I had a Bob Marley poster on my college dorm room wall.

- I've seen the movie *La La Land* three times.

IN EARLY 2022, I was on the subway and several Black and Brown teenage boys came onto the train and sat around me. And every other word out of their mouth was the N-word. It was a lot. So I took a deep breath and I very calmly pulled down my mask and said, "Excuse me, do you guys think you can teach me how to say the N-word?"

They got so excited. "You can say it! You can say it!"

I tried saying it.

"Nigger," I said.

"Nooooooo! You gotta keep it casual, keep it loose, like, what's good my nigga?"

"What's good my nigguhh?"

I guess I sounded like I was singing it. After a few more attempts, they told me I definitely shouldn't say it. And honestly, I felt vindicated. I'm fine with it. I don't need to say the N-word. Where would I say it? When I'm shopping at Ann Taylor Loft?

The Immigrant-to-Basic-Bitch Pipeline

'LL NEVER FORGET the moment I knew things had gone too far. It was during a Zumba class at Equinox. Of course, signing up for a Zumba class at Equinox should have been my first clue.

Zumba is for people who can't dance. People who need rules. People like me who can't twerk but who *can* do the Twist. And the Sprinkler and the Shopping Cart and the My Little Pony. My favorite kind of dancing is where the moves are either clearly identified in the song, i.e., the Electric Slide, or when they're barked at me from the front of the room by a white woman who has more rhythm than I do.

My ancestors practically invented rhythm, but I couldn't clap on the ones and threes if my life depended on it. Is it ones and threes or twos and fours? Doesn't matter, I can't find any of them. I was grateful that this Zumba instructor was showing me the way.

Then, out of nowhere, she tells us about a new section of our Zumba class called "freestyle." During this section, we were supposed to just . . . dance. This new section of Zumba was where we could "show our personality." And I didn't agree with this at all. This was antithetical to everything both I and Zumba stood for.

But there was no stopping it. Fifteen minutes into class, the instructor yelled, "Okay, freestyle! Let's see that personality!"

I thought to myself, *Ma'am, we're in a Zumba class at Equinox. None of us have any personality. I'm in head-to-toe Lululemon and drinking out of a S'well water bottle, I clearly can't think for myself.*

And so I did the only thing I could do: the Macarena. And as I saw myself doing the Macarena damn near perfectly in that Equinox mirror, I knew it was time to get help. And that's when I found out about the immigrant-to-basic-bitch pipeline.

WHAT IS THE IMMIGRANT-TO-BASIC-BITCH PIPELINE?

The immigrant-to-basic-bitch pipeline is a disturbing national trend where immigrant women who come to the United States young enough will adopt the basic bitch principles popularized by mass media, thereby becoming shells of the layered women they were intended to be.

IS THE IMMIGRANT-TO-BASIC-BITCH PIPELINE REAL?

The immigrant-to-basic-bitch pipeline is very real. Let's face it. We've known about it since the day we met Kelly Kapoor on *The Office*. From her obsession with banal pop culture to her devotion to a fuck boy named Ryan to her name, Kelly: Miss Kapoor is the definition of an immigrant turned basic bitch.

WHO BENEFITS FROM THE IMMIGRANT-TO-BASIC-BITCH PIPELINE?

Capitalism, obviously. Mass consumerism. Shein and other fast-fashion apparel stores. White men with podcasts.

WHO IS AT RISK FOR THE IMMIGRANT-TO-BASIC-BITCH PIPELINE?

All immigrant women.

JOIN US. THIS THURSDAY IN THE GYM.
NO STARBUCKS.

THERE WERE ABOUT 10 OF US black and brown women in the gym that day. Seated on folding chairs in a circle. No Starbucks. Our host, Ashley, an older lady with tired eyes, began the meeting.

"Welcome to the support group for immigrants turned basic bitches. Remember, we are all unique here."

"We are all unique here," everyone replied in unison.

"Let's welcome our new attendee," she continued. "Welcome, Sarah."

"Hi," I said. "It's good to be here."

"Do you want to tell us your story?"

"My story?" I asked.

"Yes. Tell us why you're here."

"Okay," I said. I cleared my throat. Ahem.

"Well, I was born in Jamaica, which is cool. But my name is Sarah, which is basic. And I feel like those two things pretty much cancel each other out. I wish I could be irie, you know? It's all I've ever wanted to be."

"We all wish we could be irie, Sarah."

"But no one named Sarah is irie. And neither am I. I didn't even have a name for the first few months of my life because my parents thought I was going to be a boy. And they had a kick-ass name picked out for me—they were going to name me *David*. But when I came out and I was a girl, they were stumped. They didn't know what to call me."

"No woman, no name!" one of the other women sang like Bob Marley.

"Exactly. Then, at some point, a family friend picked me up and instinctively called me Sarah, and I believe . . . at that moment . . . the ghost of a basic bitch named Sarah moved into my body and gentrified my whole personality."

"Ooo, a ghost story?"

"Shh, Hillary," Ashley hissed.

"Because when I was little my mom would cook the most amazing jerk chicken, but it was way too spicy for me. She'd ask me why I wasn't eating. And I'd be like, Mom, my mouth is on fire right now. And she'd say, Yuh know, Sarah, there are children round de world dat all de get fi dinna is bread an wata. And I'd be like, That actually sounds really good, Mom! Yeah, if I could get a scone and a chai tea latte, that would be amazing."

"I could so go for a chai latte right now," Hillary whispered under her breath.

"My bad taste has followed me everywhere. I'd go to a barbecue place in Atlanta and order the chicken fingers. I'd go to a burger joint in New Orleans and also order the chicken fingers. Mom would make jerk chicken, oxtail, curried goat, callaloo, plantains . . . and I wanted chicken fingers chicken fingers chicken fingers."

Ashley handed me a tissue.

"I had basic bitch taste in everything, including music."

I opened my Kate Spade purse.

"That's my purse," a woman said.

"Oh, my bad." I grabbed the right purse and pulled a few crumpled sheets of paper out of it. "This is something I found in an old shoebox. It's a transcript of an intervention staged by my five white male coworkers at IQTV in 2004."

The transcript said:

ADAM: Sarah, could you come to my office for a moment?

ME: Okay.
(Walks into office)

ADAM: Hi, Sarah.

MORITZ: Hi, Sarah.

KEITH: Hi, Sarah.

JEFF: Hi, Sarah.

BARRY: Hi, Sarah.

ME: What's . . . what's going on here?

ADAM: Sarah, we have to talk to you about a serious problem.

ME: A problem with *me*?

ADAM: Yes.

ME: Okay. What is it?

ADAM: Well, it's your iTunes playlist.

ME: What? What's wrong with my iTunes playlist?

ADAM: Well, it sucks.

ME: No it doesn't!

ADAM: Sarah, you have almost no songs and the songs you do have suck ass.

ME: I like my songs!

(Adam goes to his computer and opens my playlist, named "Sarahtonin Reuptake Inhibitor")

ADAM: Sarah . . . Bob Seger?

ME: What's wrong with Bob Seger?!

KEITH: Ace of Base? Poison?

ME: I like Ace of Base and Poison!

JEFF: "Who Let the Dogs Out"?

ME: That's a great song!

ADAM: Sarah, your playlist has no focus. Everyone has a specialty. Mine is hip-hop. Moritz and Keith are alternative rock. Jeff is classic. Barry is house. You have no specialty.

ME: Well . . . why can't my focus be music I like? Other people like my music, too. Someone is always connected to my playlist!

KEITH: Actually, Sarah, we have a computer that runs upstairs that no one uses, and we connected it to your playlist just so you wouldn't feel left out.

ME: Oh.

MORITZ: Perhaps your focus can be reggae, you know, since you're all Jamaican and stuff.

ME: Okay, I'll put some Bob Marley on there.

MORITZ: No no no, like REAL reggae.

ME: What?

ADAM: Sarah, I'm sorry. You leave us no choice. We're kicking you off the iTunes music server until you fix this problem and provide something worthy to the group.

I folded the paper and put it away. Ashley cleared her throat.

"It should be lost on no one that Sarah, a proud Jamaican woman, was ridiculed and shamed by five basic white dudes."

"ELITIST HIPSTER BASTARDS!" one woman screamed.

"Calm down, Tiffany."

"Tiffany! I picked out my engagement ring at Tiffany! Of all places. I knew I wanted a cushion-cut diamond because that was the ring chosen by the bachelor on the most recent season of *The Bachelor*."

"I did that, too!"

"Same here."

"Me too."

"After I said yes, I posted a pic on Instagram, holding up my hand to show off said ring."

"As is Instagram custom!"

"That's the whole point of getting engaged!"

"Tracey, Sheila, this is about support, not encouragement."

"Sorry," Tracey and Sheila said.

"We did engagement photos around New York City, in the back of a cab, on the High Line, under a subway bridge, and in front of weird-looking doors—"

"For the texture," Sheila said.

"Yeah. We had a black-and-white-themed engagement party at a seafood restaurant. I chose the black-and-white theme myself, and it never once occurred to me how weird it was that an interracial couple was having a black-and-white-themed engagement party. Years later I'm still wondering why no one called me on this."

"Friends and family often have trouble speaking up."

"We got married on the beach in Puerto Rico, because that's where we met at a Google offsite."

"The location you picked for your wedding was based on what your product area could afford for a team-building event?"

"Yes," I whimpered.

Ashley took a deep breath.

"Okay, Sarah. Tell us about the ceremony."

"Do I have to?"

"Only if you're ready."

I hesitated.

"We, uhm, got married at the side of a pool. I had to walk in my wedding dress with my father through the pool area. Where kids were jumping into the water and screaming and splashing like nothing else mattered, like they were on vacation or some shit."

"Sarah, they probably *were* on vacation."

"We had a whole crowd of complete strangers watch our wedding in their bathing suits! These people were not on my Pinterest vision board!"

"Own your anger."

"You know what else wasn't on my Pinterest vision board? The priest we hired, who I found on Google, who I'd never met before in my life, and who showed up hungover, looking like Nick Nolte in a Hawaiian shirt, and thought it was okay to be sitting on a stump behind the altar, smoking a cigarette, while I was walking down the *fucking* aisle. I saw him there as I walked down the aisle with my fucking father and he looked *bored*. HE LOOKED BORED AT MY WEDDING."

"Do you know why he looked bored, Sarah?"

"Why?"

"Because your wedding was fucking boring."

Everyone cringed.

"Keep going. Tell us . . . about your vows."

"Well, we did write our own vows," I said with some pride.

"What were they?"

"Uhm, I think I still have them memorized . . . I said, 'Steve, I mean, Jeff. My favorite definition of true love is this. If at the end of your life, God tells you that you get to live it all over again and asks if you choose to do it with the same person, you say yes. And, Jeff, I would choose to live my life with you over and over again, every single chance I got. If I could live a million lives with you, I would.'"

Ashley paused. This was worse than anything she'd heard before. "You did a name joke at the top?"

"Yes. I mean, it did get a laugh."

"And where did you get that definition of true love?"

"I, uhm, I read it in a book?"

"You read books?" Holly asked excitedly.

"Okay fine, I stole it from this guy I used to have sex with."

"And the 'live a million lives' part?"

". . . I think it was a Backstreet Boys song?"

One woman began sobbing.

And then it all came pouring out of me.

"We did a sand ceremony because it was only like fifty dollars extra and seemed cool. It could have been a satanic ritual for all I know. There was a vial of silver sand and one with blush sand (which was more like an orangey red and dark gray), and I poured in the blush and he poured in the silver. And the sand flowed together. Into this vase, this thin, wavy vase. And it was a symbol of us. How we were like, separate, but now we're like, together forever, you can never separate us, it was like, metaphorical and shit. And they sealed it up with wax and we carried that vase of sand back to New York and everywhere we moved. I was so scared that if anything happened to that vase of sand it meant the end of us. But it never broke, it just slowly kept losing sand every time we moved. Until, finally, one day, we were divorced and I was cleaning out the closet and found something wrapped in paper and accidentally dropped it and it was the vase of pink and gray sand and I am still fucking cleaning that shit up. How's that for metaphors, you wedding sand ceremony upseller assholes!"

Now everyone was sobbing.

Ashley took a deep breath and encouraged others to do the same.

"Now, I know that was triggering for many of you, but it was so needed and so important to see the havoc that being an immigrant turned basic bitch can bring. Let's thank Sarah for her bravery—"

"Wait. There is one more thing," I said.

Ashley looked at me with terror in her eyes. "What is it?"

I paused.

"After the ceremony, we obviously had to get photos of us walking hand in hand on the sand, because when I basic bitch, I basic bitch hard, don't fuck with me. Our bridesmaids and groomsmen stood in a line and . . . and . . . and we . . ."

"Say it, Sarah."

"I can't, I can't."

"Say it."

"We . . . we . . . we took a jumping picture on the beach."

Tiffany put her hand on mine. "It's okay. We all did."

"THAT DOESN'T MAKE ME FEEL BETTER!"

Ashley stood. "I wasn't going to do this today, but I think it's necessary."

She handed out airplane tickets to each of us.

"Through the basic-bitch-to-immigrant pipeline, basic bitches can take a trip to their homelands for three months to rediscover themselves. A quest to tease out what is *you* and what is *basic* and what is the *difference*."

We all silently stared at our airplane tickets.

I meekly raised my hand.

"But . . . is there like, Starbucks there?"

Here's an Ergonomic Chair to Protect Your Body While Your Soul Is Dying Inside

DON'T THINK I was always meant to work in tech.

When I was very little, I loved drawing characters and giving them names and writing stories about them. I was obsessed with this cartoon about rich white kids called *Beverly Hills Teens* and I wanted to make a cartoon just like it.

But then, much like the episode of *Mad Men* where their first computer arrived, our first computer arrived. Big monitor connected to a tower that my dad installed down in the basement in a small room off to the side of the staircase. And I was fascinated by it. We only had two floppy disks:* WordPerfect and Quicken. So I'd write stories in WordPerfect and then I'd write million-dollar checks to myself in Quicken. But somehow I still had no money. It was very confusing. And also a good foreshadowing of my life as a writer.

In middle school, I got my own computer, in my own room, with my own subscription to America Online. I'd go into chat rooms and share my age, sex, and location. That was the internet before the internet was the internet. And I couldn't get enough of it. AOL was where I met Jim Carrey. Can you believe it? Jim Carrey was just

---

* I'm not going to tell you what floppy disks are, you're gonna have to google it, you spoiled brats.

hanging out on America Online with the handle JimCarrey098376 and he was talking to *moi*, a 13-year-old girl, on AOL. And it was definitely Jim Carrey, don't think it wasn't. Why would he lie? We chatted about his latest films and talk show appearances and he seemed really into me. I became convinced I was in a relationship with Jim Carrey. There was a good month of my life where I was sure I was going to marry Jim Carrey.

In high school I got into PaintShop Pro, and then at the University of Maryland I fell in love with Photoshop. During my final semester, I took an astronomy class and a graphic design class. And I decided to kill two birds with one stone by focusing my graphic design project on the lessons of astronomy. I ended up getting an A in graphic design and a C in astronomy. I went on to get a master's degree in information design and technology at Georgia Tech. I worked with Dr. Janet Murray on a thesis project called "Reliving Last Night," an interactive movie where the "user" follows a woman on a date and gets to choose what she wears, what she drinks, and what music she dances to, which would then determine who she woke up with the next morning. It was loosely based on my own life.

MY FIRST TECH JOB was at Yahoo! in 2006. I worked at Yahoo! when Yahoo! was *Yahoo!* The holiday parties were awesome. You'd walk in and there'd be a band, a Christmas tree, and a table full of blow. Of course, years later, everything got so politically correct you couldn't have the Christmas tree anymore.

I didn't know it at the time but I was working in Silicon Valley during its best years. The height of the tech boom. A time when it felt like anyone could be the next Mark Zuckerberg, and that would be a *good* thing. I went to a conference where some dude named Biz presented his new website for sharing snippets of your life. It was called Twitter and it sounded so stupid. Tweets? Really? You think people who have any self-respect are going to send *tweets*? Get serious.

Everyone wanted to come up with a great idea and start a cool company and have a big party and get on *TechCrunch* or *Mashable* or *Valleywag*. I came up with ideas, too. Like a tool called the Freebie List where you could put the five celebrities you were allowed to sleep with if you ever ran into them. On my list was John Krasinski and I don't remember who else. I had another idea for a website that would give you personalized recommendations based on both you *and* your boyfriend's preferences, a revolutionary technology I dubbed "collaborative filtering" that aimed to solve all the arguments I had with my boyfriend about what to eat for dinner. I came up with an idea for a website that would let you upload yourself dancing the Soulja Boy Crank That dance and then play your video side by side with other people doing the same dance. Did I literally invent TikTok? Yes, yes I did. Where's my money? I also came up with an idea called Hyperlocal, which would tell me if there was ever a parade in my neighborhood because I hate parades but I never know when there is one. To be honest I'm still holding out for one of these ideas to come through. Any kind of investor/engineer who wants to come on board, please let me know. My burn rate is very high.

Other people had more success with their ideas. I discovered a video-sharing site called YouTube, where I'd watch videos of John Krasinski. A blog-making site called WordPress that I used to create my own blog to share a demo of my Crank That dance idea. A user-reviews site called Yelp that I never really got into for some reason. A DVD delivery service called Netflix, which is how I was able to watch the first season of *Arrested Development* on my commute from San Francisco to Santa Clara.

When I turned 30 I decided it was time to leave tech and pursue my dreams in entertainment (more on this in Part 3: Humiliation). I moved back to Atlanta and started doing stand-up comedy and then moved to New York to become the next Chris Rock. Within a year I was broke. So when my former classmate Molly Stevens recommended me for a job at Google, that paper looked real good, son.

The first step in the interview process was to design an app to rent bikes. Also known as a sneaky way to get free app design. Next, I had a full day of interviews. During the first interview I presented my portfolio to about eight people. They asked me if I was properly prepped for my presentation. I said, "Yes, I was told to present my work with an interpretive dance." Everyone laughed. I was in there like swimwear. And by "in there" I mean I'd given up on all my dreams again.

I joined the Google Docs design team, under a brilliant researcher named Antonella Pavese. And I was back in tech.

EVERYONE ALWAYS ASKS ME if it was it fun to work at Google. And I always say yes, it was fun. I knew I was having fun because they kept telling me how much fun I should be having each quarter or else I would be fired.

We did have a lot of fun, though. Our director, Fuzzy Khosrowshahi, would make margaritas at five. There was alcohol everywhere. Someone had a bread maker next to his desk and made bread for everyone like once a week.

The office was so creatively designed. There was a library at the end of one floor with huge secret rooms hidden behind moving bookcases where I went to take naps. Our cafeterias rivaled the best restaurants in the neighborhood and everything was free. There were games, and massages, and haircuts, and Kool-Aid. Lots of Kool-Aid. You had to drink the Kool-Aid. Everyone got an ergonomic chair and a standing desk so we could protect our bodies while our souls were dying inside. We could sit *or* stand while our souls were dying. It's the only OSHA-approved way to murder your soul.

There were microkitchens everywhere. Those are kitchens that sound small but many of them were bigger than any kitchen I'd ever seen. Microkitchens were these always-open food amusement parks where everything was fully stocked and it was all free. Every beverage you could imagine. Candy. Chips. Nuts. Fruit. Yogurt. Cereal. All the cereals. Every kind of milk. Bite-size grilled chicken and cheese cubes in a little plastic tub, for some reason. An espresso machine. Another espresso machine. And all this was mere steps from your desk. And if one microkitchen didn't have your favorite chips, you'd go to another one down the hall and another one on another floor, and just do that all day. And if you never find your favorite chips then you file a ticket so that food services will stock your favorite chips and then a week later, boom, there they are: your favorite chips! Microkitchens were freakin' magical. One morning I came into the microkitchen and a food worker was *pulling grapes off a stem one by one and putting them into a big, beautiful glass bowl, which she would later put in the fridge for us.* I'm sorry, Gen Z Googlers, there was no way this could last forever.

But working at Google wasn't always a bowl of handpicked grapes. For instance, there was a sparkling water tap in the microkitchens, but sometimes the water wasn't that sparkling, you know? Like, it was only a little sparkling, so it might as well have been flat. And one time, one of our gourmet cafeterias served lobster tail for lunch, but the lobster tails were, like, too big? Or the time a sushi chef came but each person was limited to six pieces of sushi at a time. If you wanted more, you had to *get back in line*. Ridiculous. The heated toilet seats were always too hot. The free massages were always on some floor that it took forever to get to. And of course, the time they took the entire Google Docs team on a trip to San Juan, Puerto Rico, which was really great in theory. But the truth was that the lawn chairs on the private beach at the resort we were staying at were just not that comfortable. Too low to the ground. Very unstable. Really hard to lean back in.

IN TECH, I WAS KNOWN as a consensus builder. That means I wouldn't share ideas of my own but I was good at taking your idea, and your idea, and your idea and making a new crappy idea out of it. Fuzzy said this was a great trait to have, but I was dubious. No one is jealous of someone else's consensus-building skills, someone's ability to hide themselves so much that everyone likes them. Strong leaders aren't consensus builders. Like you'd never see a mob boss go, "So Jimmy ratted us out to the Feds, and I think we should take him behind the dock, break his legs, and throw his body in the river. But uh, what do you guys think? Thoughts? Questions? Concerns? Big Tony, pull up the PowerPoint, let's get a brainstorm going. We'll put a pin in anything that doesn't directly relate to Jimmy's body. I'm looking at you, Sal."

I always felt fake at work, like I was putting on a show. But I think everyone is putting on a show at work. You go to meetings and you have to nod and seem engaged and make people think you care about next quarter's goals when you don't give a shit about next quarter's goals. It's a performance. That's why at the end of the quarter they give you a performance review. To let you know how convincing your performance was. And if your performance wasn't convincing enough, maybe you need to find a new role under a new director. My performance reviews always went well. Antonella would always say, "Sarah, you seem so passionate and engaged in your job." And I'd take a deep bow and say, "Thank you! That's what I was going for."

We were all considered "individual contributors" at Google. Sure, we were on a team, but we were also in direct competition with each other, which seems contradictory, and it is. We were stack-ranked as part of our performance reviews—which meant they put everyone on the team in order of contributions. We'd get a rating that went from Superb, to Exceeds Expectations, to Meets Expectations, all the way down to Needs Improvement. At first, I would always get Exceeds Expectations because no one really expected anything of me, but by the end I was usually Meets.

MY EX-HUSBAND AND I fell in love at work. Some people say if you marry someone who works 10 feet away from you, that's like settling. But I think it's more like giving up. It's like, you're here, I'm here, I can see your calendar. This feels convenient. I see you're free Tuesday night, we could do something then, or if not, I'll just see you all day Tuesday. Meeting a guy at work is better than online dating. If you meet a guy at work, you know he has a job. You know exactly how tall he is. And your first interaction with him isn't a dick pic, unless you work at Uber or something. I wasn't scared about dating a coworker, I was more scared about dating *another* coworker. Yeah, I was a bit of an office slut. But if I was a man they wouldn't call me an office slut, they'd call me a high performer. One of my coworkers accused me of sleeping around the office. I didn't know if they were referring to the coworkers I was dating or all the naps I was taking. Turns out it was both. I guess I've just always had a thing for work, and men at work, and sleeping.

So why did I leave Google? That magical place? Well, I read one of those articles that said you should quit your job and follow your dreams. So I quit my job. But then I found out those articles are written by people who want your job.

I owe my whole career to the internet. Google kept me afloat when stand-up wasn't paying the bills. And my biggest successes in entertainment have been from going viral online. But the internet has jumped the shark. Every website has 18 pop-ups. I'm accepting cookies on a minute-by-minute basis. News is nonsensical clickbait. Even if you wanted to read the article, you can't, it's covered in ads. Our apps "learn" about us, and they learn it all wrong. You accidentally click on one video about the Kardashians and suddenly you are in a Kardashian-only internet hell. And of course, there's the destruction of our democracy, and the decimation of our mental health, especially for young people and especially for young girls. And worst of all, tech keeps "redefining" things to the point where we now have just what we had before but worse. We're paying a monthly fee for every streaming service and now they're showing us commercials, too. THAT'S JUST TV. THAT'S WHAT WE HAD BEFORE. Do you know how many apps I had to install and how many accounts I had to create just to watch the Oscars last year? A LOT. God, I sound old. Remember when we weren't scared that all the stuff we were doing on the internet was going to be fed into a chatbot to replace us? Those were the good old days [takes old-timey pipe out of mouth].*

Google's first motto was "Don't be evil." Which I think was their first mistake. Why didn't they make it "Be good"? How did they come up with "Don't be evil"? When Larry or Sergey started building Google in their garage did they *start* to be evil and keep slapping themselves, like, dammit, why do I keep *almost* being evil? And then they had to remind themselves so many times to not be evil that they figured they better print it out and put it above the door, Ted Lasso style, and then make it the entire motto of their company? This motto 100 percent admits that they are capable of evil things. I mean, yes, it's transparent and true for every corporation, but it's not great for a brand. Applebee's motto isn't "Don't spit in the food." (Or is it? I've never worked at Applebee's.) But the even bigger result of this motto is that it gave other companies a blueprint for how to beat Google. Companies like Facebook and Twitter saw "Google: Don't be evil"

---

* This bit brazenly stolen from Seth Meyers.

and said, well, it's pretty clear how we're going to differentiate. And they became as evil as possible. Although if you're a corporation with shareholders, you might have no choice but to be evil, as long as it's profitable. The point is, do I wish I had sold one of my videos as an NFT and possibly made a million dollars? Yes, yes I do. But then I'd feel bad for the person who now owned a worthless NFT. But what about me, huh? What am I supposed to do with all this Dogecoin?

IF I WAS GOING TO create a social media app right now it would be one where every post you make disappears after about five minutes. Because usually within five minutes I don't even know if I agree with what I just posted. I've already changed, I'm already a new person. Does this video of a blind puppy learning how to walk really represent me anymore? No. It represents the me from five minutes ago. And everyone would get 10,000 followers and the bots would say nice things to you and connect you with people who are real and similar to you and can help you. And if you accidentally clicked on something, the internet would not try to make it your entire identity. These companies have so much info on us, they could use it for good, to make us healthier and better! Like a dating app with *no photos*. You tell us what makes you laugh, and we give you five phone numbers of people who laugh at those things too and you watch those things together. A chatbot trained by great interviewers like Conan O'Brien and Jimmy Fallon to ask *you* questions when you can't sleep at night, for people who are quiet like Rachael, and also for me to feel like I'm on a talk show.

I wish we could make the internet a happy and helpful and healthy place. Or else let's just pull the plug on the whole damn thing. Except for Google Docs. And FaceTime. And Wordle. My mom, my sisters, and I need our Wordle.

This Is Your Brain on Ganja

I SUPPOSE IF THERE'S ANYTHING truly Jamaican about me, it's that I love getting high. I started getting high a few years ago, when it was recommended to me as a stress reliever by Gwyneth Paltrow. Thank you, Gwyneth, for getting me back in touch with my Jamaican roots.

But I don't smoke ganja, I order sour apple gummies on an app. And my Jamaican family is adamantly against weed. They think it's dangerous.

In college I put up a poster of Bob Marley smoking a blunt on my dorm room wall. When my dad saw it, he asked me if I knew what that was, *that* being the blunt. I played dumb.

"A cigarette?" I said.

"No! That's ganja! Stay away from it!"

But I did not stay away from it. I got high in college. But only once. I took a few hits from a joint my high school boyfriend Andre brought to my dorm room and I was flying. Then the two of us, along with two of his friends, got in a car and drove around College Park. We stopped at a Burger King drive-thru and ordered burgers. After the bag of burgers was handed to the driver, the driver passed it to me in the back seat for distribution. This involved me reaching into the bag, pulling out a burger, opening it up to see what it was, and giving it to its rightful owner. But I was high. And hungry. So I opened up the first burger and wow it looked delicious so I took a huge bite even though it wasn't mine. Then I wrapped it back up and handed it to the dude riding shotgun.

"WHAT THE FUCK? THIS BURGER HAS A BITE TAKEN OUT OF IT!"

"My burger has a bite taken out of it, too!" Andre shouted.

"Mine, too!" the other guy yelled.

"Really? Mine was fine," I said, chewing.

They were about to turn around and head back to the Burger King and rip someone's head off, so I finally had to come clean.

OVER THE YEARS I did more of the drugs.

In my late twenties, I tried cocaine for the first and last time while living in San Francisco and working at Yahoo! The guy I was dating presented me with a tiny mountain of powder wrapped in tinfoil from god knows where. And he asked me to snort it with him. I thought my love of chalk dust in grade school would give me some proclivity toward the whole white powder thing, but it did not. After we did the cocaine or however you're supposed to say it, we went to a club, where I ran into my cousin who I spent Thanksgivings with in Maryland but who I hadn't seen in a decade. I was at the bar, which had a mirror behind it. And in the mirror I saw this beautiful Black man standing next to me. At first I was like, who's this beautiful man! Then I turned and it was my cousin. Like, a real cousin, not just someone my parents made up. We hugged. I didn't even realize he was living in San Francisco. He introduced me to his girlfriend, I introduced him to the cokehead. Then I went back to the cokehead's place to have some of the worst sex of my life. Who the fuck would invent a drug that makes you horny but unable to have sex, I'll never know. I guess I could look it up but I won't. It didn't help that I couldn't stop thinking about how I ran into my cousin and I should call my cousin and I can't believe my cousin lives here. I never did the cocaine again.

When I was 34, I did acid on an offsite in San Juan, Puerto Rico, that by now you've already heard too much about. Oh yeah, we were team-building, alright. It was me and two coworkers in a hotel room, them telling me not to eat but me being so hungry I couldn't not eat, and then it kicked in and I felt sick but then I felt great. We walked around the resort and paintings were coming to life. I ran into a VP then ran quickly away from him. I went back to my hotel room and stared at a towel for an hour, I could see each little fiber swaying. I always wanted to try acid again, but getting some for myself involved going to a weird location on the dark web and paying in Bitcoin and I didn't have the attention span for that.

And then I came back to weed. At the ripe old age of 41 I became reacquainted with the wonders of THC, which was now conveniently in Rice Krispies Treats form. Although I wouldn't try the Rice Krispies Treats if I were you, unless you enjoy projectile vomiting because you ate too much because it's so delicious and you forgot it has 250 milligrams of weed in it.

I don't think my family realizes how banal weed is now. I mean, my drug dealer's name is Terry, and he also does my taxes. The scariest thing about my drug deals is calculating the gratuity. If we want people to stop doing drugs, they should just put me in an antidrug campaign. Hey, kids, I'm a single, 45-year-old woman who spends all day on her laptop in a onesie. YOU DO NOT WANT THIS LIFE. Or do you? You don't.

YOU KNOW WHAT kind of danger I got into when I started getting high in my early forties? I'd obsessively register for MasterClasses. That's right, weed drove me to *extreme adult online education.* You might think I'm wasting my money taking these classes high, but the truth is, when I'm high, I feel like I really *could* play tennis like Serena Williams.

The other thing I love doing when I get high is getting a massage. That's right, weed drove me to *extreme self-care.* The massage place I go to is called Four Seasons Massage (no relation to Total Landscaping).

I had this great Chinese masseur, but I didn't know his name. And I didn't know how to ask because I was always high when I went there and I didn't want to look like a racist old lady who can't pronounce a foreign name. So I hatched a plan. I would hand him my phone with the Notes app open, and I would point to it, and I would say, could you write down your name? The plan was foolproof. A few weeks later, and after my massage, I took my phone out, opened the Notes app, handed it to him, and very slowly said, "Can you write your name?" He looked at me and said, in a plain Midwestern accent, "My name's Jesse." I was so embarrassed that I started to pretend *I* was the one who couldn't speak English. "Jess—ee?" I asked, feigning confusion. I pointed to my phone and forced him to continue writing it down.

"S? And then? Another . . . S?" I said slowly.

The thing I love the most about being high, though, is that when I get high, I hear subtext. Oh yeah, weed drove me to develop *extreme listening skills*. When I'm high, I hear what people are really saying. I hear emotion. I see metaphors and shit.

The first time I heard subtext when I was high was when I was hanging out with my friend Emily and her boyfriend Tanner. Emily and Tanner started talking about their dog, Pepper.

Tanner said, "Pepper pretends to care but he doesn't really. He's not a very empathetic dog."

Emily quickly agreed: "I know! It's like he's always crying wolf!"

And as they continued talking, I realized they weren't talking about Pepper at all—they were talking about each other! Tanner was calling Emily unempathetic and Emily was calling Tanner the boy who cried wolf! Dude, when I'm high I'm a genius. Couples talk about each other through their pets. This is not an observation anyone in the world has made before. And I only had to wait an entire year for the confirmation of this genius.

Emily and I were hanging out at my place when Tanner called to tell her that something terrible had happened, but not to worry, the house was fine and Pepper was okay. She begged him to tell her what happened.

Finally, he relented. "My best friend got into a fight with his girl-friend."

And Emily angrily said, "But is Pepper okay? Why the fuck wouldn't Pepper be okay?"

Tanner started crying.

And then they broke up. And I saw it all coming because of my ganja-induced superhuman listening skills.

So there you have it, kids, the dangers of getting high: online education, self-care, and listening. If you ever see me in an online associate's degree program at a silent meditation retreat and paying uninterrupted attention to you, you'll know I've hit rock bottom.

My absolute favorite thing to do when I'm high, though, is write. This book is brought to you by my brain on drugs. My high self has no filter and she's the best writing partner I could ever have hoped for. So smart, so relaxed, so good at listening to herself.

Aw, thanks.

Oh wow, when did you get here?

You took an edible an hour ago.

Oh, right, I forgot.

(Sorry, Mom and Dad.)

Sibling Rivalry

'M JEALOUS OF MY BROTHER. He's been drinking a Long Island iced tea for 25 years. Not the same one. A different one. It's his favorite drink. You know how they say if you stick with one drink for the night, you probably won't get sick? Try sticking with one drink for 25 years. You'll never get sick. Right? I'm pretty sure that's how it works. But I could never do that because I get bored of things so easily. I'm a fickle gal, and even when I know what I want, I'm too scared to say it, and I talk myself out of it and it's a living nightmare. We're still talking about alcohol, I swear. I went through a vodka phase, a Zima phase, a phase where I tried things like White Russians and Goldschläger and Irish car bombs, a malt liquor phase where I relished drinking 40s out of brown paper bags (don't ask) before settling on red wine, then white wine, then red again, before falling in love with Moscow mules and then finally realizing I can't take the hangover anymore and I have stopped drinking altogether. Once, I got George to switch to a Moscow mule. He gave it a shot, but after one round, he was back on that LIIT game. I marvel at the consistency. Consistency is so hard for me. But not for my brother. Married for 25 years, two kids, been in the military since right after high school. His clothing can be divided into military-related apparel, or USA-related apparel, or Jamaica-related apparel. And jeans. That's it. George has always known who he is and he's always been proud of it. He doesn't hesitate to ask servers for their recommendations. If you go out with my brother, there's a good chance you'll hear him say, "Between the pizza and the burger, which one would you say is better?" I'm terrified of my servers. I always feel awkward being served anything. But George makes conversation with anyone and they're instantly best friends. Last year he was temporarily stationed in Colorado Springs for training. I went to visit him and when I showed up at the hotel and told the woman at the front desk I was staying with George Cooper, she screamed, "GEORGE IS YOUR BROTHER?" She was overcome with excitement. "Your brother is AWESOME!" She would not shut up about him. He'd been there a week.

I'm jealous of my sister Charmaine. She considers herself a prolific inventor of products other people later invented. She fully believes she invented flavored water because once in the seventh grade, she put some orange juice in a glass of water. She also claims to have invented Tex-Mex chili, because one time in the seventh grade she added corn to her chili. She also says she invented neon-colored nail polish when, in the seventh grade, she used a highlighter to paint her nails. I asked her what was going on that she had so many inventions in the seventh grade. She told me she was on a roll. I love that she truly believes this. She is so delusional and so am I, but the difference is she doesn't think she's delusional. I think it's this same delusion that leads Charmaine to invent novel uses of common phrases. Her "mistakes" are my treasures. Once she interviewed for a job, but she didn't get it. Four months later, after they fired the person they chose instead of her, they called to offer her the job. And she turned it down, saying she didn't want their "sloppy seconds." This is not even remotely the correct use of this phrase. Charmaine doesn't travel, but she reads a lot and seamlessly plays off what she's read as her opinion. Like once I told her I was thinking about going to Costa Rica and she goes, *Ah, Costa Rica, it's a hidden gem, and very affordable.* Charmaine has never been to Costa Rica but everyone thinks she has. And she's okay with that.

I'm jealous of my sister Rachael. She always takes her time.

When we go out to dinner, she'll just stare at the options. Forever. And you know what, she's right to! There are a lot of freaking options out there. It's overwhelming. She's probably taking the normal amount of time someone should take. You should see Rachael get ready to eat breakfast. Not eat breakfast. *Get ready to eat* breakfast. She'll first put out the box of cereal, whether it's Cheerios or Honey Nut Cheerios. Then she'll walk away. She'll take a little stroll around the house or perhaps go back to her room. Then she'll come back and put out the bowl. Then she disappears again. Half an hour later, she puts out a spoon. And she's gone. Later, she puts down her vitamins. And then finally, at long last, sometimes up to an hour after she's started, she sits down to eat breakfast. Me? I always feel like if I don't get everything done immediately, I'm screwed. Not Rachael. Rachael is also very secure in her choices. Several years ago, she had two gerbils, and she named one George, after our older brother, and the other one Michael, after her favorite singer, Michael Jackson, and George and Michael had absolutely no relationship whatsoever to the artist George Michael. She made that very clear. This was very reminiscent of the two parakeets we had when we were little, Anderson and Cooper, years before we knew who Anderson Cooper was.

I'm jealous of my brother because he's a leader. And a father. And a partner. And it seems like he knows everyone. If you go out anywhere in his neighborhood, everyone knows him by name. I'm jealous of my sister Charmaine and how much she knows about the human body. She knows how a defibrillator works. She knows how to do CPR. She's saved lives. Bodily fluids don't make her squeamish like they do me. She's an amazing cook. She knows sign language. She is endlessly supportive of me and has watched every video and every audition and read every blog post. She's met Obama and worked with Dr. Fauci. And I'm jealous of Rachael because she never remembers her dreams and thus never spends any time telling anyone her dreams. She told me it's just silent and black when she goes to sleep. She doesn't seem to have this running monologue in her head like I do. It sounds so peaceful.

George always cheers me up. Charmaine makes me feel like I can do anything. Rachael always listens and makes me feel at peace even if she has no idea why I have to go to Dublin to meet up with an Irish dude. Again, she makes a good point.

We're all so different and I'm so glad for those differences, but it's not gonna stop me from wanting to be more like them.

This is for you, George, Charmaine, and Rachael. Because I love you. Because you continue to teach me everything about who I am as a partner and a collaborator. And also because I'm going to need you to take care of me when I'm old because I don't know what a 401k is.

My Mother's Wisdom Comes Mostly from HomeGoods Décor

AFTER MY DIVORCE, I remember finding out I wasn't going to get child support. We don't have kids, but I still wanted child support, you know? I wanted inner child support. And so I was crying and crying and hugging my mom and she hugged me back and said, "Sarah, don't sweat the small stuff. And guess what? It's all small stuff." And I was like, "Mom . . . that's the sign above the couch." I turned around and pointed it out to her. "Did you just read that to me?" That's when I realized that my mom is just like the guy at the end of *The Usual Suspects*. She's just been reading the HomeGoods décor around the house to give me advice.

Once I called her and said I didn't know if I'd ever get married again. She said, "Sarah, you have to dance like no one is watching." And I said, "Mom, are you in the guest bathroom right now?" And she said no but then she launched into something about footsteps in the sand and I know that's the framed print above the towel rack!

Another time I got emotional was when my ex said he'd signed a lease on a new apartment. He'd be moving out at the end of August. That was the moment it felt real. Like, really real. I imagined running into him, perhaps five or 10 years from now, seeing him and our dog, Stella, and they'd look older and different, and I'd barely recognize them. And the thought of it devastated me. To be so close to someone then become strangers is one of the saddest things. And I called my mom, and she said, "Time heals all wounds." I was like, "Mom, are you in the sitting area at the top of the staircase right now?"

Time heals all wounds...Which is not even true. Hashtag not all wounds. Also, this phrase really places time in the hero position when time isn't doing anything at all. We're the ones waiting around in pain for time to *pass by*. And when we're in pain, it passes slower, and when we're having fun, it passes quicker, irrefutable evidence that Father Time is a worthless asshole.

When I called my mom to tell her I'd lost custody of my sweet cockapoo, Stella, she said, "Sarah, when the tough gets going . . . I mean, the tough is going to get going . . . let me call you back, I'm in the car." I'm pretty sure she was trying to read a bumper sticker.

But whether the saying was sitting right in front of her in the form of a book, or a plaque, or a bumper sticker, or not, my mom has always been fond of sayings.

When I was anxious about something, she'd say, "You'll cross that bridge when you come to it."

When I was mad, she'd say, "That's just the way the cookie crumbles." Now she was coming for my dessert.

Once I heard her talking to my aunt Bev about a wayward cousin:

"Birds of a feather flock together," my aunt said.

"It's all about the company you keep," my mom replied.

"Misery loves company," my aunt said.

When I was a kid, my mom would comb my hair, and it was always knotty and it always hurt, and she'd say, "Beauty feels no pain." Which is truly a Jedi mind trick of gaslighting and dangerous patriarchal indoctrination.

When I broke up with John in college, she said, "That which does not kill us makes us stronger." Which doesn't change the fact that whatever it is, it's *trying to kill us.*

One of my mom's sayings might be the reason I got a divorce in the first place. Six years into wedded bliss, my mom called to wish me a happy anniversary. And then she said, "You know, Sarah, the seventh year is always the hardest. It's the seven-year itch."

"Mom, that's a movie, not a real thing," I said.

But she insisted it was true. She said her hardest year with my dad was the seventh year. And only later did I realize I was born around the seventh year of their marriage, *which I figured out because I can do math, Mom.* Four months after she cursed me with her knowledge of a Marilyn Monroe movie, I was asking for a divorce.

Years earlier, when I told my mom that Jeff didn't seem happy and I thought maybe he was going through a midlife crisis, she said, "Is he getting enough sun?" Yeah, I thought. That's what our marriage was missing. Vitamin D. When my mom isn't giving me wisdom from HomeGoods, she is recommending sun. She truly believes it's the cure for everything.

My mom suffers from seasonal affective disorder, which made moving to America especially hard. She knew it would be cold, but she didn't realize there would be so much less sun. And so she decided to buy a sun box. I think she found out about it from someone at work, but I like to imagine that it was a door-to-door sun box salesman, who knocked on the door of a Jamaican family who'd literally just moved from Jamaica in the dead of winter. My mom opens the door and the salesman says, "Do you miss the sun?"—and she drops to her knees as if God has answered her prayers. "Yes, mon, me miss the sun like crazy!" It was that salesman's lucky day. Then again, maybe the sun box company was tracking a database of recent immigrants from sunny countries and knew where to find us. Either way, my mom bought two sun boxes: one for home and one for work.

EACH MEMBER OF MY FAMILY reacted differently to news of my divorce.

My sister Charmaine insisted we try therapy again, because she is a romantic who believes in love and wants to be married herself.

She made the most beautiful speech at our wedding. She planned and hosted my parents' 50th wedding anniversary. But I told her I refused to be fired by another therapist. Charmaine said she didn't realize you could be fired by a therapist, and I said neither did I. How do they fire you? Well, after about 12 to 15 sessions, they say something like, "I'm not sure I can help you," and you never hear from them again. Your problems are so bad they won't even pretend to help you just for the money. Charmaine was really disappointed. I wondered if maybe she'd already bought our seven-year anniversary gift. It was probably engraved and she wouldn't be able to return it. Speaking of, if any of you are in the market for some "Jeff & Sarah" engraved knickknacks, please reach out.

I spoke with Aunt Polly. I hadn't visited her house since she moved to Florida, and she said she had a wall of photos of all the married couples in the family. I told her I was getting a divorce and she said, "Well, I guess I have to rearrange this mural again."

"Oh, I'm sorry, Aunt Polly," I said.

She sighed. "It's okay, I've done it before."

When I told Rachael I was getting a divorce, she said, "Oh, okay."

When I told my nephews, they said, "Cool."

My dad had a lot of advice for me.

One of my favorite things about my dad is when he asks you a question, he'll never leave the burden on you to answer it. He'll do it himself. When I was married to Jeff, my dad would call and ask the same three questions. How's the weather. How's Jeff. How's the job. And he'd answer them all for me.

DAD: How's the weather? It's about sixty degrees and sunny, right?

ME: Yeah, that sounds right, Dad.

DAD: How's Jeff, I just talked to him, he just got promoted.

ME: Nailed it again, Dad.

DAD: How's the job, Mom says you're busy?

ME: Yeah, pretty busy.

About 30 to 60 seconds later, he'd say, "Love, my honey, say hi to Jeff." Eventually he added, "Tap Stella." But that was a big move for him. At first, he didn't say anything about Stella because in Jamaica dogs are animals, they do not have cute outfits and health insurance. But eventually she was added to the conversation lineup. Then I got divorced and lost the dog and now we have less to discuss.

There are two things my dad loves to talk about. One is God. The other is money. Two things that've always gone together well, historically speaking. I don't mind discussing God, but I really have to be high for that. Money I absolutely cannot stand talking about. There's no thrill in making more money for me, there's only relief. Like when this book sells 100,000 copies, I'm not going to be like, hell yeah, I'm rich. I'm going to be like, wow, I made like two dollars because the publishing industry is so fucked up. But if I sell like a million copies I'll be like, cool, now I can relax for a bit. I can sleep in more than usual. All I want is to live a simple life at the top of a Marriott with room service for the rest of my life. But I will never get to do that because I'm bad at money. I don't understand money. I mean, seriously, what is depreciation? My father's explained it to me so many times and I still don't know. I'll never know. Is the stock market even real? What is this voodoo that our entire culture and society is built on? But my dad? He loves the stuff. Studies the stuff. Is very good with the stuff. Investing. Stocks. Bonds. Real estate. Moving money from one place to another to take advantage of introductory offers.

When I bought a townhouse at age 28, my father was instrumental. Mortgages, down payments, fixed rates, lump sums, dim sum, he knew it all. And when I moved to San Francisco but couldn't sell the house because the market had just crashed, he helped me become a landlord. Walk-throughs, credit checks, rent checks, knobs, fobs, blobs, repairs, replacements, he handled it all. He always helped me with my car. He always had advice on the best savings accounts. And he always helped me do my taxes. I never really had to understand depreciation because he understood it for me. I always had so many questions for my dad because I never understood anything, and he understood everything.

However, I no longer own a house or a car, and I started using Quicken to do my taxes. I think he might've been a little disappointed when I did that. There you go, Quicken, ruining my life again.

But he did give me some advice as a newly single woman:

1. Get a Taser.

2. J.Lo and Alex Rodriguez are separating, so are Bill Gates and his wife.

3. Your mother doesn't want a gun in the house, that's why I haven't bought one.

4. Get a Taser. You can write it off.

5. Anytime you want you can hop on the iron bird and come on down here. You can work from anywhere and you have your family to support you all the time, okay, sugar pie?

6. You know I told you about this Taser thing. Make sure you're well trained.

I FaceTimed my brother to ask for advice about my marriage. He was at home and had just gotten off a Zoom conference call. And he was in his camouflage fatigues. I was pretty tickled by this. They had to wear fatigues on Zoom calls? I was like, what are you hiding from, bro? Can they even see you? Does a military Zoom call look like no one's there? He died laughing at this, even though it's not that funny and I'm already ashamed of it.

I told my brother I was thinking about leaving Jeff.

"What? Why? Are things kinda rocky?" he said in his signature upbeat voice. I think he might have even danced a little when he said it.

"Uh yeah, bro, things are 'kinda rocky,'" I said sarcastically. "They're a little bit kooky. They are far from hunky-dory."

He asked about therapy and I told him we were already on our third therapist.

"Oh, so it's not your first rodeo?" he asked.

"Uh no, bro, not our first rodeo," I said.

Then my brother suggested working on a sort of performance-improvement plan with Jeff. Ask for specific changes. Figure out how to measure success. Create a timeline. See what the results are.

"You both have to put one hundred and ten percent in. It takes two to tango."

Now that I think about it, I don't think George ever got off his military Zoom call.

FOR MY MOM'S BIRTHDAY THE NEXT YEAR, I got her a plaque that says, "It is what it is." I got it as a joke because it's the most cliché, overused, cringe-inducing phrase in the book, not this book but most books. I thought she'd laugh. Instead, she loved it. She hung it above the mirror in the hallway next to the powder room. But at least now when I call her and she says, "It is what it is," I know exactly where she's sitting.

The Prodigal Daughter

IT WAS THE SUMMER OF 2021. I was no longer going viral, I was now going through another divorce. I'd just moved back in with my parents. And it was mango season.

Now, I've never been into mangos. I remember watching the mango episode of *Seinfeld* and wondering why Kramer was so into fruit all the time. I've had a few good apples here and there, but I never saw the crazy appeal of fruit, especially with mangos and especially enough to get banned from a grocery store for it. But that summer I became a changed woman. A mango woman. I started to love mangos almost as much as my mom did.

My parents have three different mango trees in the backyard of their tropical Florida paradise. They are so self-sufficient. They wanted mangos, so they planted mango trees—so smart! I never would have thought to do that, and even if I did, those trees would've been dead while still shrubbery. Each mango tree made a different type of mango that had a different sweetness and texture and consistency, and my mom loves all of them.

Through the kitchen window, I watched Mom and Dad pick mangos using a long metal stick with a basket attached to it. It was Mom's job to point out which ones to pick and Dad's to use the stick and bring them down to the ground. Then they'd pack them into brown paper bags and put them on the floor of the pantry. When they were ripe, my mom would devour them while standing over the kitchen sink. And this is the first time I discover my mom's happy place.

Since I was actively going through a second divorce, I found myself marveling at my parents' 52-year marriage. Mine lasted six. I hated thinking about it. I cried a lot and soothed myself with edibles—secretly. And being secretly high around my family at the age of 43 while going through a divorce was an eye-opening experience. It was like I was seeing them all again for the first time.

One evening, the four of us—me, my dad, my mom, and Rachael—were eating dinner when Rachael pointed to the backyard. We all turned to look, and there it was: a giant iguana. My mom screamed. If her love for mangos is at one end of the spectrum, her hatred for lizards is at the other. I'm pretty sure that's how spectrums work. I do have a degree in economics.

So then my father, Lance, Sir Lancelot we'll call him, jumps up and practically sprints to the garage.

"What is he doing?" I shouted.

"Getting the slingshot," Mom said ominously.

I was scared. I was very high and in no way prepared to watch an iguana slaughter. But Dad was gone. It's like he'd been waiting for this moment his entire life. Suddenly he reappeared in the backyard, standing about 10 feet away from the iguana and preparing his slingshot. My mom, Rachael, and I watched him through the kitchen window, standing out of our seats, angling for the best view. It's like we were watching *Jurassic Park: Retirement Home*. It was a reverse David and Goliath that would definitely not be sponsored by PETA. My father pulled back the sling and launched a silver ball. He missed. He tried again. He missed again. We sighed. Finally, one silver ball hit the iguana in the side of the head. The iguana blinked. That went on for about 10 minutes, with my dad making contact here and there and the iguana acting like maybe it was raining. Finally, the iguana just slowly slunk away into the lake, unbothered and unharmed. The movie was over. We finished up dinner. My dad returned the slingshot to Amazon.

THERE WERE LOTS OF AMAZON PACKAGES arriving that summer. Inside one was a giant fake rock my mom ordered, which is something I had no idea you could buy. She was redesigning the garden in the front of the house, and she knew all that was missing was a giant rock. We took walks around the neighborhood to see what others had done with their front gardens. There was one neighbor in particular who Mom was convinced was stealing all her gardening ideas. Mom pointed out this house, annoyed. "See, they copied my fountain. See, they copied my pavers." She would get annoyed, but she would do it, too. She'd stop in front of a house and collect intel on the types of plants, rocks, and trees they were using. And that's how she decided she wanted a giant rock. When it arrived, it looked like it weighed 100 pounds, but it barely weighed 10. It was like the papier-mâché rocks I had to paint for the set of our high school production of *A Midsummer Night's Dream*. As my mom was figuring out where to put the giant rock, she'd pick it up and move it around over and over again. From the neighbors' perspective, here was this 72-year-old woman lifting a giant rock like it was nothing. I'm sure they thought she was on drugs. But she wasn't. I was.

As soon as she found the perfect spot for the rock in the front of the garden, a small lizard decided that this rock was *its* favorite morning spot. Its tail had been cut off, in what appeared to be some kind of lizard-on-lizard related incident. And as much as my mom hates lizards, she got used to this one. She even liked him. She named him Fred. I'd go out there some mornings and see her working on her garden while Fred was sunning himself on the giant fake rock.

Most mornings I woke up early and took a walk around the neighborhood listening to an audiobook about confidence. Because that's what I decided I needed. Confidence. I was going through a divorce, and trying to finish writing an audiobook, and pitching two TV shows, and my confidence in myself was spent. I needed confidence to stick with this divorce and see it through and not change my mind. Confidence onstage. Confidence to make decisions about my projects. But there's nothing that will make you feel like a bigger loser than listening to an audiobook about confidence.

It was on one of those walks that I came across a dead baby bird on the sidewalk. It was small and blue. I started crying. I decided right then and there that I was a vegetarian, because that seemed to be the thing to do at the time.

I went home and told my mom that I was now vegetarian.

"Is it because your friend Katie is a vegetarian?" she asked as she got out her vegetarian cookbook, because that's just the kind of supermom she is.

"No, Katie's not a vegetarian."

"Oh. Is she a lesbian?" My mom is also bad at segues.

It's at this point I realize my mom has been waiting to ask this question since I told her about my new friend Katie, who was really instrumental in me realizing I needed a divorce. Probably since that moment, my mother has been wondering if Katie and I were in a relationship.

"No, Katie's not a lesbian." I laugh.

My parents have always been suspicious of my friends. I think it's an immigrant thing, it was always safer to stick to family. Maybe that's contributed to my own suspiciousness in friends and my lack of having friends and my being bad at friendship. I start to wonder if my mom thinks Katie and I could only be close if we were having a sexual relationship, and then my mom says: "I've thought about being one."

My brain stopped.

"What?" I said.

"I thought about being one. I did try to be one for like a month or so. But your father didn't want me to be one."

I was so high I was like, Holy shit. Is my mom telling me right now she tried to be a lesbian?

Then she goes, "And so we started eating meat again."
Oh.

THROUGHOUT THE SUMMER I realized that as my parents aged, Rachael had slowly become the only person in that house who knew where anything was. She has a photographic memory. She knows Wi-Fi passwords by heart and can figure out pretty much any electronic gadget. For my parents' 50th anniversary a few years earlier, I wanted to get them one of those life-size cardboard cutouts of them on their wedding day (because I'm original and have original ideas). But the picture I needed to scan was in Florida and I was not in Florida, I was in New York. So, over the phone, I walked Rachael through scanning the photo on an old, giant scanner, hooked up to a Windows machine, at the right DPI and saved as the right file type, and then emailing it to me. It was so complicated. But through the miracle of FaceTime and Rachael's eternal patience, we did it. And it arrived in time for their 50th wedding anniversary party at a nearby hotel, where it was propped up in the lobby and was a huge hit on Instagram.

After the party was over, they took the cutout home, but my mom was never happy with any spot it was in. She kept moving it around the house and it started to pop up in random places and terrify me around almost every corner. Sometimes I'd just look up and there it was, giving me heart palpitations. My 26-year-old dad grinning widely in a smooth black suit, holding my mom's 19-year-old wrist, her smile framed with a white veil. Every time I saw it, I was haunted by this fairy-tale wedding and this picture of a successful marriage, and it was my own damn fault for ordering that thing on Etsy.

SOMETIME AROUND THE MIDDLE of the summer, my parents had to go to a funeral. And my mom spent several days deciding what to wear. She narrowed down her options to two different black dresses. She modeled the first one. She walked back and forth behind the couch and did a little catwalk turn. She had accessories and shoes on, but no bra, so she told me to picture her with a bra.

"Which one you like?" she asked.

"Both," I said. They really did both look good.

And then they took off for North Carolina for a few days, leaving me alone with Rachael. While they were gone, there was a huge storm. I cried over Jeff, and Rachael just looked at me. I'm sitting there, bawling, crying, and she goes, "Are you okay?" and I laughed and said, "No, Rachael, I'm obviously not okay." And she said, "Okay." And went back to the game she was playing. And I couldn't help but laugh.

Rachael stuck to a strict schedule. That night I asked her to sit and talk to me while I finished my dinner. But she didn't talk to me. All she did was stare at the clock. Right in front of my face! And then she yawned loudly. And it didn't seem like a real yawn. I had never known Rachael to be a pretend yawner.

"Was that a real yawn?" I asked.

"It could've been," she said.

"Could've been?" I said.

"Some yawns are more real than others."

I swear Rachael is like Jamaican Yoda. I've spent my whole life trying to get inside her head, trying to really understand her. But that summer I realized I'll never be able to. Even if I could put myself in her head, *Being John Malkovich* style, it would still be *me* inside her head. One of the most painful parts of my childhood was seeing my father punish her, usually for making mistakes in school. I felt so angry and helpless. The only thing I could do was make her laugh. But now she was the one making me laugh.

When my parents got back from North Carolina, my mom was frazzled. They were driving in the rain and they didn't know quite where they were going and my father's moods are notoriously volatile on the road. His moods reminded me of Jeff's moods. I guess I always knew I married my dad, but it wasn't until that moment that I wondered . . . was my mom married to my ex-husband?

My mom made it work, though. But me? Sometimes I wish I'd never even tried. I was upset about my marriage falling apart, but the real bummer was how much I missed while I was obsessed with men and getting married. How my marriage took me away from my family, instead of bringing me closer to them. I felt like I didn't know my parents, I didn't know Rachael. My brother visited us that summer with my sister-in-law, Susie, and my nephews, Ryan and Tyler. My nephews were in high school now. I'd missed their whole childhoods. I realized I didn't remember what we did for my brother's or sisters' 40th birthdays. They turned 40 and I don't even remember it.

On the way to Florida that summer, I met a man on the plane and gave him my number. He texted me. It quickly turned romantic. My divorce papers were barely written, much less signed, and here was another man for me, ready and willing. But I realized that it was the last thing I wanted. I realized I'd lost so much time already to men. Looking for a man, trying to keep a man, cleaning up after men, placating men, and I just felt actually completely finally done. Also he was really bad at sexting. I blocked his number and I turned my attention back to my family. And I noticed so many things that summer:

- My mother doesn't leave the house much, but when she does it's usually to go to the doctor, and she must do her hair and look nice and put on makeup. It's like a special occasion.

- My father's phone beeps constantly—he has an alarm set for everything: go to the bank, take medication, do something with the pool.

- If Daddy buys bananas and any of them go to waste, Daddy will get very upset and swear he's never buying bananas again. This is the first time I realize that's why Mom is always baking banana bread.

- If you cough, my dad will tell you to drink fish oil.

- If you walk barefoot, my dad will tell you to put on some slippers. And drink fish oil.

- My dad threatens to haunt my mom when he's dead and she begs him not to. This sounds like a cute conversation but it is very, very serious.

ONE DAY, RACHAEL, MOM, AND I watched a momma goose leading her baby geese along the edge of the lake. And a smaller, slower baby goose was getting left behind. Rachael became sad for that baby goose. "Oh no," she muttered under her breath. "Oh no."

But then the momma goose went back to help the one who'd fallen behind, and my mom said, "See, Rachael, she's going back for him. She'd never leave him." And I saw Rachael nod, reassured.

And I excused myself to go cry in my bedroom.

I was really high.

PART 2

Determination

I Lost My Virginity to a
Guy Named Brad

I WENT TO THE ZOO the day I lost my virginity. Or should I say, we lost our virginities. There we were, just two lovesick teenagers on a Sunday afternoon at the Smithsonian's National Zoo, holding each other in front of a giraffe. A loudly peeing giraffe. That kept peeing. As we kept holding each other.

There was something animalistic in the air. And in our loins. And we took our animalistic loins home with us. Specifically, his home, to his bedroom, where we could hear the sitcom his parents were watching just outside the door. Canned laughter has done it for me ever since.

Brad and I had been talking about the possibility of having sex for a long time. I liked that it would be the first time for both of us—seemed like an easy win for me: I wouldn't be compared to anyone. I never expected to enjoy it. It was more about giving him a present. A present he'd spent the better part of the previous two years asking for.

Brad and I met in Drama Club during my sophomore year of high school. It was kind of a fluke that I ended up in drama at all.

When I first got to high school, I didn't want to do Drama Club. I was going through a phase I like to call my "I'm going to be a cheerleader and date a hot football player like they do in the movies" phase.

But I didn't make cheerleading and none of the football players liked me, so I did Poms (the far less exclusive dance team) and went after a hot basketball player named Andre instead. I knew how to pivot, and so did he.

Andre was a young Kobe Bryant type with a mischievous grin and a carefree attitude. I saw him at a game, and it was love at first sight. For me.

Andre was considered the ungettable get of Magruder High School. Or maybe I just told myself that because he was ignoring me. I was undeterred. I made my crush known throughout the halls of second period and my gym teacher came in with the unlikely assist. She asked Andre if he'd ask me to go to Homecoming with him. And he said yes to her and I said yes to him, and my dad gave me $40 so I could pay for my own meal, so I wouldn't "owe him anything." The limo showed up. He gave me a corsage. We had a magical night. But I had to be home by 11 p.m. and Andre didn't like that. And after Homecoming he started ignoring me again.

Mom told me not to chase him but I was impatient. I'd get up the courage to call him but the second someone else picked up I'd lose my nerve to ask for Andre and ask for his brother instead. Soon I was in a semiserious, phone-call-only relationship with his brother. And Andre was somebody else's boyfriend. That's when I decided I didn't want to be a popular girl. Mostly because it wasn't really working out. I quit Poms and gave up on Andre, and suddenly a new opportunity landed in my lap: being a slave. Specifically, a slave in the Magruder Drama Club's production of *The Miracle Worker*. They were in need of some sort of Black people and I sort of was one! And my days of trying to be cool and wearing Guess jeans and Quiksilver turtlenecks were over. I was now a Drama girl. And that's where I met Brad a year later.

BRAD WAS A SWEETHEART. He was beautiful, Italian, and best of all, completely in love with me. By then I was a sophomore. He was a freshman. I'd watch him working on our set for the spring musical, *Leader of the Pack*. He looked so good with a hammer. He had a nice butt. So when he asked me out on a date, I didn't think twice. We spent an entire Saturday afternoon together. We got dropped off at the mall and walked around and got on one of those giant water tricycles on the man-made moat outside Cheesecake Factory and then we saw *Hot Shots! Part Deux*. We laughed hard and held hands.

After getting picked up by his mom, we were back at his house lying together in a hammock on his back porch and I was so impressed that I'd spent so much time with one person and I wasn't bored. I don't remember for the life of me what we talked about. I just knew we were going to be, you know, official. We couldn't get enough of each other.

Our first kiss came a week later at Jessica's house for the spring show wrap party. It was late (like eight o'clock) and we were in the backyard. We walked off on our own. And he told me to look up at the stars, and I did. And when I looked down, his face was right in mine. And we kissed.

Brad introduced me to Stone Temple Pilots. And Pearl Jam. And Led Zeppelin. We came up with names for our future children. Our first child would be named Led Zeppelin. That kid would be almost 30 today and probably hate me.

Brad and I went to prom together. He showed up in a limo with a corsage *and* a box of my favorite cereal at the time: Lucky Charms. But he wasn't getting lucky quite yet. He had to prove his love for me. Cue Madonna.

Brad's displays of affection were often sweet but always tragic. Like, once on a snow day he decided to walk the whole four miles from his house to mine. When he finally got to my house, my parents were already home from work and strongly suggested he call his mom to pick him up. Oh, and he got the flu.

Another time, we went to Burger King after rehearsal, and they were giving away free glass jars with their kids' meal. Offhandedly, I said I'd love to see what that jar looked like smashed to bits. As we're walking out, Brad takes his glass jar and throws it high up into the air, and it falls onto the parking lot into a million little pieces. It was pretty cool. What was not cool was the cop parked nearby who charged Brad with vandalism, which landed him in a courtroom where he was ordered to serve 24 weeks of community service. Oh, Brad.

Brad and I learned to drive together. We took this awful driving class every day after school with an instructor named Mr. Johnson, an older gentleman who loved his transparencies on his overhead projector. What kept me awake was when I noticed he'd always start or end his sentences with "at any rate." I told Brad. He said he'd noticed it, too. We winked every time Mr. Johnson said it, which was a lot. In the corner of my notebook I'd add a tick each time I heard him say it. It was often upward of 25 times in a single one-hour class. Excruciating. A few months later, we both passed our driving tests but had some trouble with speeding tickets. Turns out the rate you're going is pretty important, Mr. Johnson.

A FEW NIGHTS before the big night, Brad called me to tell me he got condoms. Well, a condom. And I said okay, and something cute like "soon," probably, I don't remember that part. But I do remember this next part.

Brad goes, "I got a boner about you tonight."

Which was way more explicit than I'd ever heard him be.

"What?" I said.

"I got a boner about you."

"Okay ... great."

"I want to show it to you."

"Uh, sure."

"Yeah. It's pretty long."

"Oh ... okay."

"I wrote your name across the top."

"What? . . . That's weird."

"Why's that weird?"

"Why would you write my name on your penis?"

"What? What are you talking about?"

"You said you got a boner about me tonight."

"No, I WROTE A POEM about you tonight."

"Oh. Yeah, that makes more sense."

So we were gonna have sex. All we needed was the perfect moment. And that moment came after we got back from the zoo. We were in his room. The lights were out. He locked the door. Sure, we could hear his parents watching TV outside the room, but I told him I was ready. And I lay down on his twin bed. *Oh man, I think they're watching* Laverne & Shirley. He got a condom out of the very back of the very top shelf of his closet. *Laverne is so funny.* He got on top of me and somehow we figured out the rest.

A few seconds later we were outside waiting for Charmaine to pick me up. He asked me if I had an orgasm. I laughed in his face and said no. Man, I was such a badass bitch. *You'll spend the next fifteen years lying about this,* I whisper to my 16-year-old self through time and space.

As we saw Charmaine turn the corner, we decided we needed a nickname for what we just did, since we could never say the word "sex" out loud anywhere. We liked the double meaning of "Sunday" and "sundae," and since it was a Sunday and we loved getting sundaes, we'd nickname sex "sundae." We agreed we would have another sundae soon.

Alas, it was not meant to be. As soon as I got home, my mom hurried me into the powder room. "Something's different about you, I can tell! What happened? Tell me what happened!" She wasn't messing around. So I told her that Brad and I had sex. And she pulled me close, got up in my face, pointed a finger at me, and said, "NEVER DO IT AGAIN." *Sheesh, Mom. It's just sex,* I thought. But my mother put the fear of God in me, and Brad and I only had one more sundae after that. It was in a field around the corner from my house. We both got poison ivy. Poor guy. He was always waiting around for the possibility. But I was very, very afraid of sex. It didn't help that every time we were alone in the basement, Rachael would appear. At the time, I thought it was because she wanted to hang out with us, now I'm wondering if Mom kept sending her down there.

Brad and I broke up in my senior year. I don't even remember why. Maybe I got tired of Led Zeppelin. I filled that void with trying to be a cool popular girl again. Student body vice president. Homecoming committee. And going to senior prom with Andre, who was back in town from his first year in college.

That's where I had sex with the second person I ever had sex with: Andre. I asked him to senior prom. My parents let me stay out late. My mom had told me not to have sex with Brad again, but she didn't say anything about Andre! We went back to his house. His family was asleep so we grabbed a blanket and we went out to the cornfield next to his house because I obviously didn't learn my lesson about outdoor sex. We started having sex. And I had my eyes shut very tight because I was trying very hard to have this orgasm thing everyone was talking about. So I was really concentrating. But man, I was starting to get a headache. So I opened my eyes just to take a mental health break and I saw Andre, with his eyes wide open, just looking around the cornfield.

And I was like, "What are you doing?"

"Trying not to come," he said.

And then he came. And I was like, lemme get this straight: I'm trying to come and I can't and you're trying not to come and you do? If that isn't the patriarchy, I don't know what is.

BRAD AND I CROSSED PATHS again at the University of Maryland, where we both did drama for a while before I changed my mind about it again. After college, he worked at a theater, met an actress, and they got engaged. I asked if I could come to their wedding, he said no. I'm not holding a grudge or anything.

Andre and I got back in touch in college, and later while I was in grad school. By that time, he had an apartment, and a dog, and a digital scale to weigh drugs. I thought, *Wow, me and Andre are going to end up together after all.* But one night we were on the phone talking about the next time we might see each other, and the phone just cut out. And I couldn't get him back. I kept calling but couldn't get in touch with him. And I never heard from him again. The truth is, his name isn't even Andre.

Brad and I are still in touch. He and his wife and his mom came to see me do stand-up a few years ago.

So yes, I lost my virginity to a guy named Brad, but at least it was a good Brad.

Gather 'Round, Kids, and Let Me Tell You About Match.com

SPENT MOST OF MY TWENTIES AND THIRTIES looking for love on dating websites. Which means I've been on dating websites since the dawn of dating websites. Like Match.com. Whenever I bring up Match.com I feel like an old witch telling a scary story . . .

Gather 'round, kids, and let me tell you about Match.com! You see, it was this website, that's right I said website, NOT AN APP! A wehhhhhbbbsite that you went to on your DESKTOP COMPUTER! And you would pay TWENTY-FOUR NINETY-FIVE A MONTH! To match with local singles in your area!

Okay, gather closer, children, and let me tell you more about Match.com. The pictures were *tiny*. And *fuzzy*. Match.com was no place to see a clear depiction of who you were communicating with! You could barely see them! But! Instead of pictures, you had the next best thing: a 10-page essay from the individual about their wants, desires, hopes, and dreams, all displayed in a very, very tiny font. And do you know what you'd do then, children? You'd actually READ it. You'd voraciously search for any typos or unnecessary exclamation points or ALL CAPS or any sign at all that this person was a raging psychopath. BUT THERE WAS NO SWIPING. If you liked someone, you had to CLICK A BUTTON with your MOUSE that was connected by a WIRE. WE DIDN'T HAVE WIRELESS MOUSES THEN, CHILDREN!

And this, this was the scariest part, my little scribble scrabbles, because you'd often get *letters* from people you had no interest in at all—pages and pages of letters telling you everything you didn't want to know about a stranger you'd most likely never meet, some even saying that you were betraying yourself and your race for wanting to date white men—OH YES, people could SEE the ethnicities you were interested in! And make you feel ashamed of it! IT WAS HELL.

I'M KIND OF A PIONEER when it comes to online dating, which isn't something I should take pride in and I don't. I almost started teaching an adult education class on online dating, and by almost, I mean I thought about it for like a day. I've been on every dating site ever invented and even some that weren't. I often used Friendster to meet men. Men who would offer to pick me up and take me to dinner and then never show, thereby forcing me to call the restaurant only to find out there was *never any reservation under that name*.

When I moved to Atlanta for grad school, I promptly made a profile on a brand-new website called FriendFinder.com. There, I met a white rapper known as Cunninglinguist. But I never found out if he was.

On Myspace, I met a college professor who was a terrible kisser who I broke up with because I said he didn't make enough money, but if I'm being honest, and I am, it was the bad kissing.

I was on *The Onion* personals—oh yes, *The Onion* had a personals section; do they still? I don't know—where I met a guy named Bill who was the first person to give me a real orgasm. Onions have done it for me ever since.

OkCupid is where I really shined, though. Shone?

The intro to my OkCupid profile said:

> Good evening. Or whatever the case may be. And welcome to my profile. Welcome to you who has opened my profile. Anything is possible on my profile. The only limit . . . is yourself.

(This was a reference to my favorite website in the world, Zombo
.com,[*] introduced to me by the cokehead. See, it was an inside joke
test. Anyone who specifically mentioned Zombo.com in their message to me would be moved to the front of the line. The not-that-
long line.)

I went on to say:

> My name is Sarah and I am a 34-year-old web designer person
> who sometimes works a little too much and has lived in the
> city for about two years. I am a stable, responsible, only
> slightly crazy individual with Jamaican heritage and a penchant
> for using words like "penchant." I enjoy cracking myself up
> and would love to meet someone who enjoys that, too.

What other woman admitted both her dedication to work and
her mental health state in her online dating profile? I'd venture to
say none!

And it got better:

> I am here looking for a ridiculous spark. I don't have time for
> anything less. I don't believe in finding the ONE, I believe
> there are many ONEs out there, a few of which I've already
> met, so now I'd like to find just ONE of those ONEs again.
> And not fuck it up this time. Like me, you should be
> financially independent, creative, curious, kind, and cute.
> Unlike me, you should have a penis.

I dare you to find a clearer, sexier, or whhhittier explanation of
what I wanted in life. Feel free to steal this, anybody looking for
someone with a penis and using a dating app that has a place to
put text.

And to that amazing profile I'd get responses like:

---

[*] I could explain to you what Zombo.com is, but it's probably easier for you
to just go to Zombo.com. It's still up. I just checked.

> Hi, how are you doing? I hope that this message finds you in good health both physically and mentally. I viewed your profile and I must say that you're a very intriguing Women with many layers to oneself. Your one that I would like to know more about and I hope that you would like to do the same. So until I hear back from you, enjoy the rest of your weekend. By the way I'm John, and you are? P.S You have an Amazing Smile that lights up your Face when you smile. The Smile is the gateway to a Beautiful Soul.

Dating apps have only gotten more superficial and more disappointing since. Everyone's trying to stand out but they're all doing it in the exact same way. Everyone seems to have blended into the same exact person who loves "music and movies and having fun."

I miss meeting people in person. I had the best pickup lines. For instance, sometimes, I'd just go up to a cute guy and punch him lightly in the arm and say something like, "Hey, what's your deal?" Or I'd pretend to know his name. "Is that you, Mark? No? Jason? No? Jake? No? David?" It would eventually get so annoying that he'd just tell me his name. Pretty smart. Once I reintroduced myself to a guy I had given my number to three weeks earlier. He asked for my number again. I told him I already gave it to him. He didn't believe me. We looked in his phone. There I was.

Another great way we used to meet people in person was the manager game, which I coinvented with my friend and wingman extraordinaire, Alex. Here's what you do:

Put your drink and/or purse down somewhere, then walk up to a table. Say something to the effect of, "Hi, I'm Sarah. I'm actually the manager here. I just wanted to make sure that you were pleased with the service and see if there was anything I could do to make your experience a more pleasurable one. Have you tried our chicken tenders?" I did this to two tables and it was an instant conversation starter. Watching Alex do it was priceless. He went up to a table and introduced himself as the manager, and one of the girls at the table said it was her birthday. And he went, "Let me see what I can do about that," and walked away.

A few weeks later we were at it again. This time, he went up to a table and introduced himself as the manager. After he walked away, I went up to the same table and introduced myself as the manager and said there were reports that someone was going around posing as the manager and that if this happened, they should report it immediately.

Unfortunately, the real manager caught on and we were kicked out of the bar. We were fired by the real manager for pretending to be the manager. And we never actually got any dates that way.

But we had *fun*. It's so much better to meet someone in real life.

I'm not sure why I was so convinced I'd meet the love of my life online. I guess it seemed easier . . . put up a few pictures, put in your criteria, hit a search button. Using technology to fall in love seems like a smart thing to do. But falling in love is not smart. It's foolish as hell.

Pick Me, Pick Me

I N MY EARLY THIRTIES, I started doing extra work. Well, not extra work, but work . . . as an extra. On sets. You know, movies and stuff. I found a Craigslist post for extras for a Smirnoff commercial and sent them my acting résumé. And some half-naked pics of myself.

A few days later, I got the response:

hey sarah,

out of 300 submissions they have chosen 25 people, and you were one of them. the director said they will start shooting around 3PM. i know it doesn't pay a lot of money, but it's going to be a pretty cool commercial with a lot of hot boys and girls. do you think you can make it?

COULD I MAKE IT? Of course I could make it. Me, Sarah Cooper, had been selected to be an extra in a Smirnoff commercial. I was one step closer to that Academy Award.

It was a Super Bowl commercial, I think. Or NBA finals. Either way, I was dressed like a hooker. *Surely they'd have to feature me in this outfit,* I thought.

The shoot was on a Saturday at a McMansion in Buckhead. The house was gorgeous, but as extras we were relegated to the basement. Just a bunch of hot boys and girls, looking hot, with nothing to do but eat and talk to each other until someone summoned us to set. And I wasn't going to eat because I had to look good on camera, and I didn't really want to talk to anyone because I felt old. They all looked twentyish and I was thirtyish. But I also looked twentyish so maybe they were thirtyish too? It didn't matter. I had a job to do. Be the best Smirnoff extra I could be. I was going to be the Kate Winslet of extras (not *the* Kate Winslet in that scene from *Extras*, although that will always be my favorite performance of hers).

Once in a while a person with a walkie-talkie would come down and grab a few of us and then leave. Each time that happened, I'd perk up a little bit and try to look extra Smirnoffy, but it wasn't working. I was always thinking, *Pick me, pick me*, and they never did.

The hours passed by. I lost hope. Maybe I just didn't have what it takes to be a Smirnoff extra. I decided to eat something. *No use dieting now*, I thought. *My career is over*. I shoved 18 potato chips in my mouth. And that's when I saw him. Ooh, I saw him. He walked in through the out door. He wasn't wearing a raspberry beret, but he was still the most beautiful man I'd ever seen.

By that point in my life, I had stopped believing in love at first sight. But when I saw him, I felt like I understood so many things I'd never understood before, because I am a Sagittarius and a drama queen. I understood slow motion, lightning bolts, feeling like I couldn't breathe, or not that I couldn't breathe, I just didn't want to. I didn't want to move a muscle. I couldn't disturb the rarefied air. But I also felt this need to shout it out and tell anyone and everyone about this magical thing that just happened! I wanted to look at him forever. I wanted to do whatever he wanted. And I don't like doing nothing for nobody.

He crept through the basement without a word. Looking for . . . something, I'm not sure what. He was drop-dead gorgeous, so I assumed he was a model, which made me think he wasn't very smart. How very stereotypical of my thirtyish-year-old brain. Sure, I wanted him to have the intelligence to go along with the looks, but the truth was I didn't care. I fell in love before I knew his name, his occupation, or anything else about him. Forsooth! My Shakespear-

ean sonnet–level feelings were based on nothing more than his presence in the room. That's how badly I wanted to have sex with him.

And then he did something I couldn't resist: He barely looked at
me and left.

My mind was racing. *Where did he go? Would he be back? How
long has he been modeling? Would he be able to support us after we got
married? Does he plan to stay in Atlanta? Which neighborhood is he
in? Does he have a nice place? How many kids does he want?*

And just as I was lost in thought about my future with a man I
legit did not know at all, someone with a walkie-talkie pointed at
me. I had been summoned. SUMMONED TO SET.

And when I got to set, there he was. And that's when I realized . . .
he was no model. He was the director. The first director I ever fell
in love with, but certainly not the last. All directors have that na-
scent daddy energy. Like they just got off a horse.

I was melting. How was I supposed to get into character as an
enjoyer of both Smirnoff and the Super Bowl or NBA or whatever
with the love of my life breathing mere feet away from me? The
shoot passed by in a flash, and the next thing I remember is driving
home on a dark, windy road thinking I had to see him again, some-
way, somehow.

For the entire following week, I could think of nothing but him.
I had to contact him. I could not NOT contact him. But how? I
mean, I'd already found his full name, his LinkedIn, where he
worked, and his Facebook profile. But what do I *say* and which
communication channel do I *use*?

I asked my friend Shawn.

"This guy is big time, Sarah. He's all business," Shawn said after
reviewing the evidence. "And you're sitting here thinking about
weddings and babies. He'll sleep with you but he won't respect you
unless he thinks you're totally focused on your career. He's a rich,
hot, successful guy. Literally thousands of women want to trap him
into a marriage, or at least child support."

"What do I do?" I begged.

"Tell him you have a foundation for needy kids."

"What?"

"Never mind. Here's the blueprint. You send him an email. You want him to feel special, not for being hot, or powerful, but for his mind, for his merits."

"Right."

"I'll write it. Four sentences. Plus a call to action. In a separate paragraph."

And then we wrote an email that would make me seem businessy and interested but not too thirsty. I'm going to share it with you now. I recommend none of the tactics used below.

Hi Luke,

Just wanted to thank you for your great work on the Smirnoff commercial Saturday night.

(THANK YOU FOR YOUR GREAT WORK? WHAT AM I? HIS BOSS?)

I've only been on a few commercial shoots, but I noticed you had a distinctive way of directing that definitely stood out from what I've experienced so far.

(I'D NEVER SHOT A COMMERCIAL BEFORE IN MY LIFE.)

You seem like someone who really enjoys what he's doing, and I gravitate to people like that.

(GRAVITATE. GOOD ONE, SARAH.)

Forgive me for checking out your Facebook profile,

(FORGIVE ME, DADDY.)

but I noticed that you are also into writing and design. I was a lead designer at Yahoo! before leaving to pursue acting.

(WHO IS THIS PERSON?)

I think we have a lot in common and I'd love to know more about you. Give me a call at ***-***-****.

—Sarah

Can you believe he actually responded to that shit?

Thanks Sarah. I had a good time at that shoot too. Thanks for being a part of the cast. I thought you definitely stood out. I'll send you a friend request so I can check out your profile as well.

It was on. We were getting married.

He invited me over. We played pool. He wanted to have sex, but you know, I knew we were getting married, so it was better to wait.

I wanted to go on a real date. I invited him to my favorite restaurant, Houston's, where he wasn't so much staring at me as he was staring at the TV above my head with the game on. And then when the bill came, I jokingly said, "Let me get that," a little game I like to play where I pretend I'm going to pay so the guy can stop me. But he didn't stop me. He actually let me pay. And then we had sex. And I know relationships aren't a competition, but it felt like he was winning.

There were a series of trysts after that. One involving whipped cream. I didn't enjoy the whipped cream, and I wondered how hard I was willing to fight for my future husband. I decided it was a line I would not cross again.

But we had some fun conversations, too. Conversations I was compelled to mash with my fantasies and immortalize in Final Draft, which had become my favorite pastime. I encourage all of you to shoot your own version of this. Use the hashtag #Foolish-Scenes, because this one is.

———

INT. LUKE'S BEDROOM, NIGHT

Luke and Sarah have just made love for the second time. They are both a little tipsy from the margaritas. Luke has his head buried in Sarah's chest as she strokes his hair.

SARAH

Ok, so here's a dumb question.

LUKE

Shoot.

SARAH

When you go to the grocery store, and you're picking out apples . . . do you imagine that the apples are saying, "Pick me, pick me," or that they're saying, "Don't pick me, don't pick me!"

LUKE
(pause, laughs lightly)
Both.

SARAH

Both?

LUKE

Yep. The best-looking apples that are ripe and fresh are saying, "Don't pick me," because they're happy where they are. And the ones that are all bruised up and looking for an ego boost are saying, "Pick me, pick me."

SARAH

Wow. You are the only person who's ever answered that question that way.

                    LUKE
Oh, so this is an interview? You have
questions you ask everyone?

                    SARAH
No . . .

                    LUKE
It's okay. I have interview questions, too.

                    SARAH
Like what?

                    LUKE
                 (sleepily)
Oh, I don't know.

                    SARAH
Come on.

                    LUKE
Okay . . . What is the definition of true love?

                    SARAH
                 (pause)
That's a good one. I think . . . it's
when . . . your happiness is dependent on
them being happy.

                    LUKE
You read that somewhere.

                    SARAH
True.

                    LUKE
True love is this . . . When you're abducted
by aliens, and once they're done

experimenting on you, they tell you that you've earned a chance to do your life all over again, and they want to know if you want to do it all over again with the same woman . . . and you say yes.

> SARAH

Wow.

> LUKE

Yeah, I stole that from somewhere too.

> SARAH

I figured.

> LUKE

I'm sleepy.

> SARAH

Go to sleep.

> LUKE

Okay.

> SARAH

Do you believe in love at first sight?

> LUKE
> (falling asleep)

No.

> SARAH

I didn't use to.

> LUKE
> (eyes closed)

Mmm . . .

                    SARAH
                  (slowly)
But . . . when I saw you I understood so many
things that I'd never understood before. I
understood slow motion, lightning bolts,
feeling like I couldn't breathe, or I
didn't want to breathe in case I disturbed
the air in the stillness of that feeling of
being near you. I understood love at first
sight. I understood the need to shout it
out and tell anyone and everyone about
something so magical. I wanted to look at
you forever. I wanted to do whatever you
wanted. And I don't like doing anything for
anybody. I prayed you had the intelligence
to go along with the looks, but the truth
was I didn't care. I had to see you again
whether or not you did. I fell in love
before I knew your name, your occupation,
or anything else about you. Now I see why
there's nothing truer than that. My
feelings for you are based on nothing more
than your presence in a room or the way
your eyes met mine . . . as little as that
seemed to happen.

                    LUKE
                  (waking up)
You need a ride home, or . . . ?

I was completely in love with Luke, but the weird thing was—he
seemed to only want sex. It was just as Shawn predicted, despite
my business email and my ability to pay for every meal. And I
didn't want just sex. I wanted him to spend the rest of his life with
me. I would have to convert him into my boyfriend. And the way to
do that was easy. I would just have a little talk with him. About our
relationship.

He texted me at about two a.m. on a Saturday. He wanted me to come over to have sex. And I thought, *You know what? Now's a good time to talk about our relationship.*

So I called him. That's right. I responded to a two a.m. text with a phone call.

I told him that I'd like to do things with him other than sex.

He played dumb. "Other things? Like what?"

"Other things," I said. "Just things other than sex."

"Like what? Anal?"

"No, like a movie, a basketball game, dinner, pottery, a hike—just things other than sex!"

"Oh, you want to be my girlfriend?" he said.

Whoa. That escalated quickly. I backed away. *Abort,* I thought, *abort. I can't tell him I want to be his girlfriend. That will scare him away! I just wanted to do pottery with him!*

"No," I said.

"Yeah, you do. You want to be my girlfriend."

"No! You said that word, I didn't say that. I just want to go watch a movie!"

"Why can't you just admit you want to be my girlfriend?"

Now that one stumped me. So I relented. I fell into his trap.

"Okay. Yes. I do. I want to be your girlfriend." I sighed.

"Now, was that so hard?" He laughed.

"No." I laughed back.

Then came the silence. The long. Awkward. Silence. I was trapped. There was only one thing I could say now. Only one question I could ask. Only one way to go. Dammit, his Facebook profile clearly said he loves chess and here I was backed into a corner about to get checkmated or knighted or however it works and I had no moves. Dammit, why didn't I learn chess? So I said the only thing I could say.

"Do you want to be my boyfriend?"

He paused. "Nah, that's not gonna work for me."

"Why not?" I asked, completely bewildered, like a fawn in the forest about to watch her whole Bambi family get slaughtered.

He paused. "Because I'm fucking a lotta bitches right now."

I didn't really have a good comeback for that.

I headed over to his place. I stopped to get whipped cream.

CSI: Ficus

MY HUSBAND AND I GOT A FICUS. Or a rubber tree plant. I'm not sure what it was. It had leaves. It was sort of tallish. We got it at Home Depot. It looked good in the corner. But as much as I liked how it looked, I didn't like how needy it was. It seemed like I had to water it every day. And if I didn't it would look all droopy. And it was annoying. I found myself forgetting to water the plant, then remembering, and then cursing at it while I was watering it because I was late for work. Yes, I worked for myself, and I wasn't late for anything, but I still had to get going. And I found myself saying to the plant, jeez Louise (the plant's name was not Louise, that's just a saying), jeez Louise, why do you get so dry all the time?

Jeff and I had just gotten married and bought our first place together, a loft in San Francisco, and now it was obviously time to get a plant. Now, I've never been a mom and don't have much of a maternal instinct, but I was really trying my best with this ficus or whatever it was. But I was annoyed. Because I didn't think it would be this much work. And all the work had fallen to me.

I had become unpaid labor for this ficus. Maybe I should have named it Louise. Maybe if I'd named it, I would've had a stronger connection to it. I just resented that thing. And then it started dying—like, for no reason at all. I watered it. I put it in different spots. But it started to look, like, very bad. I mean, I didn't tell it that, but it must've sensed that's how I felt because I kept, like, clipping parts of it off and moving it and just generally looking at it like it was a freak. And I was frustrated because I didn't want to be emotionally invested in this thing. We got it at Home Depot. That's not even a real plant store.

I made the tough decision to put the plant outside. It was not an outdoor plant, but I guess I started to think maybe it needed more sun than it was getting inside so maybe the extra sun *outside* would counteract the harshness of the outdoor San Francisco weather for this pussy-ass ficus plant.

The plant went outside. And I'd look at it. From inside. Behind the glass door to the patio. And I liked the distance between us. The plant looked kinda sad but I dunno, for a while I thought it was starting to perk up, maybe? But then, no, no it really wasn't. Poor thing. I gave up on it and it gave up on me and it just started to really die. Yellow leaves falling off. Poor thing. *But why was it so needy? Why couldn't it fend for itself, just for a little bit?* I stopped watering it regularly. I felt guilty. And I'd get mad at myself for feeling guilty. I closed the curtains so I wouldn't have to see it. I brought it back inside for a little bit but then put it right back out because it seemed worse inside. This ficus was on its last legs. It was over. There was nothing, nothing I could do. And nothing Jeff would do because he'd already forgotten about it. It never had a chance. Not with me. I don't have a green thumb. I have two nongreen thumbs. I got a cactus for my desk at work once. It died immediately.

I never cultivated any sense of maternal wisdom. I still feel like a people-pleasing idiot when I talk to my nephews. I try to teach them lessons, but it always sounds like I'm just trying to say it in a cool way, you know? I'm like, don't do the drugs! And they're like, don't you do drugs? And I'm like, hey, let's get some mac 'n' cheese. And then George calls me and asks me to stop talking to his kids about drugs. I never feel more awkward than when I'm trying to be wise for the young ones. When young women want me to mentor them, I'm like, *I want you to mentor me. You have a business degree from Brown, I can't teach you anything.* I have no authority. No one listens to me.

It felt like this plant wasn't listening to me. I took the only next logical step. I threw it in the dumpster.

Please, don't judge me for this. I am coming to you here with shame and remorse. But I promise you, I thought it was dead. It wasn't my fault.

I put it in a plastic bag. It didn't fit in the plastic bag. It was a big ficus or whatever so it only half fit in the plastic bag. But I tied it up, its leaves and main stalk sticking out of the plastic bag. I took it downstairs to the trash room. I tossed it in the dumpster. And I didn't give it much thought beyond that. I knew Jeff wouldn't notice and I'd forget about this plant almost immediately. I gave it my best shot with Louise, I told myself. It just didn't work out and I wouldn't be getting another plant anytime soon. I picked up the pieces (the leaves that had fallen in the hallway) and moved on.

But then the unthinkable occurred.

I got an email notification about a new post to the Google+ page for our condo building. That goddamn cesspool.

This Google+ page was a place where the tenants of our condo building could passive-aggressively air their grievances to each other. It was tedious. People would complain about boxes left in the hallway, then someone would comment that this was a live/work loft so the boxes should be fine. Then someone would get out the HOA handbook and find the specific code about hallway cleanliness. Someone would get a rug and it would be delivered folded and they'd take a picture of the rug and be angry that someone did this to their rug, then someone would say, *Let's take a look at the video of the delivery,* then they would determine it was the delivery guy's fault. They were all babies. And I feel the same way about babies that I do about plants. I'm not good with them.

There was also this long-simmering war between the people who bought into the condo building when it was first built and those who bought their condos later at much higher prices and who were seen as "ruining the vibe," when the truth was, the vibe was shit to begin with (we bought later at a higher price). But I was always trying to be a good neighbor. This was our first condo as newlyweds, after all. I thought we were going to be there forever or at least until we could sell at an even higher price. I even volunteered for the Garage Cleanup Committee, which was just me and this other woman discussing how to improve the cleanliness of the garage. I fucking hated myself for volunteering for that committee.

Anyway, the Google+ notification said someone had just posted a picture on our Google+ page. And when I looked . . . it was a picture of the ficus in the dumpster. Three pictures, actually, of my ficus. Lying there. Half-wrapped in a plastic bag. And the caption said:

> Hello, I would like to propose that we not discard living plants in the dumpster. I saw someone toss this plant (a corn stalk dracaena) in the dumpster earlier today as trash. It's not trash, it's a living plant. I have since pulled it out of the dumpster and placed it upright in the trash room. It's been exposed to too much direct sunlight hence the bleached top leaves, but if you provide it with a mix of sunlight and shade and repot it into a bigger pot, it will thrive.

I couldn't believe it. A corn stalk dracaena? What the fuck is that? Also, who is this bitch? Does she not have anything, literally anything, better to do with her life than to watch me commit what is most certainly not a crime?

When I tell you San Francisco is an uppity place, believe me. Once we went to a hole-in-the-wall dive bar and we sat AT THE BAR and I ordered a BURGER and it came WITHOUT KETCHUP and so I asked for KETCHUP for my BURGER at a BAR and she said:

"Have you had our burgers? You don't need ketchup."

I was like, uh, okay. I tried eating the burger. I needed ketchup. Ninety-nine percent of the reason I eat burgers is to eat ketchup. I insisted. Finally she agreed and then disappeared into the kitchen, no doubt to check with the bar manager and the chain manager and the head of sales and the president of production and the PR guy if I could have ketchup. She came back with a bottle of sriracha ketchup. Not even real ketchup. And she put a little in a saucer for me like I was a fucking cat and then hid the bottle under the bar because she *didn't want other people to see me using ketchup on their burger that doesn't need ketchup.*

But despite the known uppityness of San Francisco, I truly thought this ficus in the dumpster thing was silly and it would blow over, and I decided to ignore the post, but then my neighbors started commenting things like, "Oh my god, who did this?" "Why would someone do that?" "Shouldn't it at least have been put in the compost bin?"

The comments kept flooding in, and everyone kept piling on. I knew we were just a hop, skip, and a jump away from someone posting a screengrab of the security footage, with me in my daytime onesie, gleefully tossing a ficus into the dumpster. I had to fess up.

I don't know exactly what I said in response, because as you know, Google+ has since shut down (shocking), but it was something to the effect of, "I'm so sorry. It was my plant. I really just thought it was dead. I did not know."

Then, that same woman commented that she would bring the plant into her own home and take care of it. She shared a story about how she'd rescued many such plants in dumpsters before. And I had no idea that "dumpster dives to save plants" was a thing someone would brag about. I guess that's considered some kind of flex in San Francisco?

And you know what, fine. Good for her. I'm glad she saved that plant and it found a home. But when she started posting updates about the plant every two weeks just to spite me, that's when she took it too far. *Here's the plant now, doesn't it look great? I gave it a new pot, it has the perfect spot in my house, it fits in so perfectly with all my other plants, it's starting to grow, it's flowering, it's so tall now! It's going to college, it's going to be a doctor,* and on and on and on and on she went. It was awful.

But I know one day that plant is gonna do 23andMe and find out who its real mother is. And when it tries to get in touch with me, I'm going to tell it the truth. I'm going to say, I bought you at Home Depot, Louise. Don't you ever forget that.

Google Docs Knew I Was Getting a Divorce Before I Did

THERE I WAS, IN A HOTEL ROOM, in LA, in April 2021, on the bed, in my underwear, blasting Usher's timeless classic "Love in This Club" from my laptop, high as fuck. What was I doing? Oh, I'm gonna tell you. I'm gonna tell you real good. I was looking for a definitive answer to the age-old question: Should I get a divorce?

You know how it is, you're married and you're unhappy, but you don't know if your brand of unhappiness is just the normal, every-day "marriage is hard" type of unhappiness, or the "wow, this is a mess, I'm wasting my life" type of unhappiness. And what better way to figure that out than Google?

This wasn't my first time looking to Google to tell me if I should get a divorce. Nope, I'd been here before. Well, not here, in LA, but in Hawaii. Three years ago. On vacation. After spending most of our vacation fighting on vacation because fighting on vacation is so much fun. Why keep your fights local, amirite? Fighting should be done in glamorous places, glorious places, expensive places. The more expensive the better. See, when you fight on vacation, you realize what true misery is. Your sour mood is in a constant battle with how goddamn beautiful everything is and how much goddamn money you spent on it, and I swear, you've never felt more alive with rage. It does what every vacation should do: make you want to go home.

As soon as we got to Hawaii, I knew we were gonna fight because this place was just beautiful. Wow, look how blue the ocean is, I bet we'll fight while watching a sunset. Wow, this food is delicious, I bet we'll fight before the dessert gets here. Wow, the hotel staff is so nice, I bet we'll fight in front of one of them. I bet it'll be Rick, he seems like the person who least deserves to be subjected to our unhealed childhood trauma. Man, I can't wait to fight in front of Rick.

So after we fight in front of Rick, we're in our hotel room yelling and screaming, well, he's yelling and screaming and I'm sitting on the bed wondering *how is this my life?*, and we go to bed angry, which we said we'd never do. I'm huddled in my corner and he's in his corner. I'm pretending to sleep but I'm actually on my phone, which I'm pretty sure is how all women in crumbling relationships go to sleep, and I do what any woman in a crumbling relationship would do in that moment, I google "Should I get a divorce?"

And the first result is a quiz, because of course it is. *Need to make a major life decision that will affect the entire trajectory of the rest of your life? TAKE A QUIZ.* So I'm like, hell yeah, I'm taking the fuck out of this quiz. I'm hoping it ends by telling me where to find a lawyer and how to write a postnup, but the quiz is a total letdown.

Is he cheating on you?
No.

Is he physically abusive?
No.

Is he unemployed / dependent on you?
No.

Does he make you do all the chores?
No.

Does he cook?
Yes.

Wait, he cooks?
Yes.

Does he have a job?

Yes.

Is it a good job?

Yes.

And he cooks?

Yes.

And what do you do?

I stay home all day, pursuing my dreams.

Results:

Bitch, you crazy. Why you think you need a divorce? This is a good man! We see from your IP address you're in Hawaii. Did he take your ass to Hawaii? Girl, you better give that man a blow job before he leaves your ass.

After that quiz I figured I must be trippin. I straight up just thought I was trippin for the entire rest of our relationship.

But then, one week before I was in that LA hotel room on the bed in my underwear, we had the Big Fight. Oh yeah, the Big Fight. It was a home game, not away. And it was our biggest, baddest fight ever. It was the UFC championship of dumb married couple arguments.

In this corner we have Jeff, and he wants the light switch on.

In this corner we have Sarah, and she wants the light switch off.

We've seen this fight before, Jim.

Yes, we have, Jim.

Wait, I'm Jim.

No, you are.

And that was us. See, we had moved from a windowless apartment to one with giant windows, because I thought maybe my mom had a point and Jeff just needed more sun. And with these giant windows I didn't think the lights needed to be on during the day, but he did, and I couldn't understand it. But this time instead of thinking I was trippin, I was like, wait, is he trippin? Wait, are we both trippin? Am I using that word right? After this biggest, baddest, most ridiculous fight in a long stream of ridiculous fights, I finally wondered if maybe my husband and I just weren't compatible. Also, we'd just been fired by our third therapist.

ONE WEEK AFTER the Big Light Switch Fight I flew to LA to shoot a CBS pilot based on a book I wrote called *How to Be Successful Without Hurting Men's Feelings.*

I hopped off the plane at LAX with a dream and my cardigan. I got to the Airbnb by 10 a.m. but it wasn't ready until four p.m. I had to wait at a Mexican restaurant *all day*. This is all so *crazy*. I order a hundred dollars' worth of weed *delivery*. (Those were the original lyrics to Miley's song.)

When it was finally time, I arrived at the Airbnb. I got an Airbnb instead of a hotel because I was trying to be frugal. I was trying to save CBS some money, I guess, ignoring the fact that Marriott runs through my veins. I thought the Airbnb would be good enough but it was just not what I pictured after looking at the pictures. It was a room above a garage. It smelled fumy. There was a weird stain on the carpet. The kitchen window overlooked an alley where a man was whistling. Not doing anything else. Just . . . whistling. It was like every Airbnb—all these rules, no music, no noise, no pets, no smoking, no visitors—oh, but the clown from Stephen King's *It* will literally be haunting you.

At this point I want any excuse to leave. Bedbugs? No. Dirty towels in the bathroom? No. Asbestos? I couldn't tell, but probably not. So I convince myself to stay. But I couldn't even get comfortable enough to take off my coat. God, I'm such a princess. I tell myself I'm staying, and I order Instacart. That guy is still out there whistling. I look and see if maybe he's doing a little dance, too, but nope. He's just leaned up against a brick wall. Whistling to no one.

I figured the best next course of action was to get high. Yeah, when you're feeling uncomfortable, get high, that's my motto. I grabbed my weed delivery, struggled for 18 million hours to get it open, then ate a pineapple gummy. It didn't taste very good, so I had another one. Then I had to figure out where to hide the edibles, because I guess as long as I live, I'll never wrap my head around the fact that this shit is legal. I hide them in the drawer underneath the TV. Yeah, good job, Sarah Cooper. No one will find them there.

Jeff calls and we argue. The Big Light Switch Fight led to us, for the first time, openly discussing the possibility of divorce. The edible was really hitting while we talked. My phone died. I looked at hotels. They seemed expensive. Then I got distracted and looked at old pictures of me and Jeff, the vacations, the apartments, the birthdays, the holidays. I start to wonder if maybe I was happy and just didn't realize it.

Then Katie called. I told her I was looking at old pics of Jeff. Having just gotten out of a relationship herself, she says, *Oh you're at the looking-at-old-pics phase. I remember that part.* Katie encourages me to look at pics of THE HOT SHOWRUNNER instead.

See, for the past few months I'd been casually mentored by a hot showrunner over Zoom. He had an amazing voice and he was handsome, friendly, generous, smart, and funny and captured my imagination in a way that I hadn't let happen with anyone else since I met Jeff. Honestly, the kind of guy I pictured for myself before I stopped picturing things for myself. And he was a showrunner. Nothing hotter than a man who runs the show. So I start googling pictures of the showrunner. *Showrunner in a tux. Showrunner in a blazer and jeans. Showrunner in sweats.* I start dancing to "Love in This Club" for some reason. And obviously now it's vibrator time. I pull it out of my suitcase and go to wash it in the kitchen sink because I'm not trying to get any weird diseases from my skeezy vibrator, I don't know where it's been, and there's the whistling man staring straight at me as I'm washing a fucking vibrator. That's when I decided I just couldn't take it and I booked four nights at a hotel.

I ordered a Lyft, packed up my Instacart groceries, closed my suitcase, put everything back in its place, turned out the lights, and started to leave when suddenly the owner of the house pulled into the garage right beneath me. But my Lyft was already waiting for me. I'd have to walk past the owners. They're going to ask why I'm leaving. *Allergies, I'll say allergies.* I leave the apartment, I'm shaking, I try to put the key back in the lockbox, but I drop it. And then my suitcase falls down the stairs. The 12 stairs. BANG BANG BANG BANG. I'm high and panicking. I run down to get the suitcase and wheel it past the owners talking in the garage . . . They don't even look at me, thank god.

I finally make it inside the Lyft. I'm breathing deeply but I'm okay. I'm okay. I've got everything. Man, I should not have tried to escape an Airbnb this high. But everything's okay. I'm a mile away from that Airbnb and closer to that sweet, sweet hotel room when I start to panic again. Do I have everything? Do I have my charger? Yes. My wallet, yes. But it still feels like I'm forgetting something. I realize how high I am. I'm just being paranoid, I thought. Thank god for that weed. Then I remember. The weed. *I left it in the drawer under the TV.*

"WE NEED TO GO BACK," I screamed.

I don't know why I didn't just leave it there. I think I thought the police would find it and arrest me for my pineapple gummies. We turned around, I had to sneak past the owners in the garage again. I got my weed, and finally, an hour later, I was safe. Safe in my hotel room.

AND THERE I WAS, on the bed, in my underwear, blasting Usher's timeless classic "Love in This Club" from my laptop, high as fuck. And my mind went to Jeff again. But I'd already taken a Should You Get a Divorce? quiz, and I failed that, so what can I do now? So I decided that instead of reading the World Wide Web I'd read the Sarah Wide Web—that is, the journals I'd been writing in Google Docs.

I've been journaling most of my life. I kept my first journal in middle school. They were blow-by-blows of my life, as well as the height, hair color, eye color, hairstyle, and general vibe of everyone I met. I'd also record how many push-ups and sit-ups my crush could do (Brook, stocky, dark hair in a skater cut, bluest blue-green eyes you've ever seen, hangs out with the popular kids; 52 sit-ups, 36 push-ups).

In my twenties, I had a blog called *The Dirty Dirty*. I was living in Atlanta at the time and that was sort of an unofficial nickname for Atlanta and I thought that was a clever name (I was wrong). Those blogs were random thoughts, stories, and some early attempts at fiction and satire, and posts that started with things like, "Well, I had to turn down the part in the lesbian werewolf movie."

While working at Yahoo! I wrote in one of many black-and-white composition notebooks I would steal from the office supplies cabinet. I'd take it to a few meetings, write in the first few pages, then leave it at home and get a new one. It was in one of those journals where I wrote, "How to look smart in a meeting, draw a Venn diagram," which turned out to be the start of my first book.

In my early thirties I had a handwritten journal—my first attempt at morning pages—where I wrote almost exclusively about what I ate, what I was going to eat, how much exercise I did, how much I weighed, and the circumference in inches of every limb.

But right around the time I met Jeff, I started journaling in Google Docs. I was also working on the team that designed Google Docs, which is where I met Jeff. It's all very circuitous and connected and incestuous (but not actually incestuous). I'd write mostly when I was angry or frustrated or sad, I'd write stand-up bits, I'd write motivational speeches to myself. And I found it very therapeutic.

But on this night in an LA hotel room, I didn't want to write, I wanted to read.

I went to Google Docs and searched "journal jeff." And there were my journals, about 40 or so, that mentioned him—many of them in 2015, the year we got married, a few in 2016, 2017, 2018, and 2019, and then a bunch more in 2020 and 2021. And I started reading.

And this part was like the ending to a movie—it turns out I'd been writing pretty much the same thing about Jeff over and over again for the past eight years.

How can I make him happy?

How can I make him happy?

How can I make him happy?

I'm not gonna lie. I was shook. I'd been going in circles for eight years and didn't even realize it. I found an unnatural, unhealthy preoccupation with *how to make him happy.* And an anger at not being able to focus on myself. I wrote about how miserable, drained, and lost I felt. My discovery of the word "codependence." Feelings of wanting to escape. And then things were okay again, and he'd make me laugh again, and the cycle would start all over.

If I hadn't been able to read it in black-and-white, without the proof that I wasn't happy and that things weren't changing, I don't know if I would've been able to ask for a divorce. Because I kept forgetting how miserable I was.

After filming the pilot, I flew back to New York and worked up the courage to ask for a divorce. I had no idea how I was going to do it. How do you look someone you love in the face and tell them you no longer want to be married to them? When I finally found the words, it was on a Zoom with our fourth couples counselor.

"Sarah, are you done?" the counselor said.

"Yeah," I said, in my smallest, weakest voice. "I'm done."

And I left.

In the Name of the Queen (Sheets)

HEAR YE! HEAR YE! *I hereby reclaim this linen closet in the name of the Queen! Sheets!*

Forsooth, this linen closet was once a house for my former betrothed's ratty T-shirts, boxer briefs, and socks; it is now the blessed home of sateen flat and fitted sheets, comforters and blankets, towel sets folded in thirds and topped with matching hand towels and washcloths. Let it be known henceforth and forevermore, forsaking all others, that this linen closet is now ... expressly, and only ... FOR LINEN.

But it wasn't always so ...

I had asked for the divorce. I'd gotten myself a lawyer. And I was back in the apartment packing up my stuff on the night before my flight to Florida to move back in with my parents. Jeff didn't want to be there, so he took Stella to a hotel for the night. I didn't know if I'd ever be back. So naturally I got high and walked around the apartment in my underwear, taking it all in, one last time. We had just moved into this place and I loved it so. It felt like a hotel, it was the home of my dreams. I walked into the kitchen. I'll miss you, kitchen. I walked into the walk-in closet. How I love closets big enough to walk into! I walked into the bedroom. Goodbye, bedroom, I shall miss ye most of all!

And then I opened the linen closet.

God, I was excited about that linen closet. It had been years since I'd had one. YEARS. I didn't even remember what it felt like! When we were taking a tour of this apartment and they showed us this linen closet, I swooned. Oh, the joy! A place to put our towels and our sheets that wasn't some weird Container Store box on top of the winter coats or underneath the bathroom sink? I was in heaven.

So you can imagine my chagrin when, shortly after we moved in, my then-husband claimed that linen closet for his T-shirts, boxer briefs, and socks. Oh, the anger. The horror. The wretched, uhm, anger.

Every day, I'd open that linen closet, see his T-shirts, and boxer briefs, and socks, and curse the day he was born. And I'd curse myself for not having the courage to tell him he should find somewhere else to put his T-shirts because this was a linen closet, goddammit! But then I'd just blame myself for taking so long to find him a dresser, because without a ready-made solution for where to put his T-shirts, boxer briefs, and socks, how could I possibly broach the revolutionary and quite controversial idea of putting LINEN in the LINEN CLOSET?

I had a six a.m. flight and I had to finish packing. But then I fell asleep while hiding weed gummies inside Blow Pop wrappers to put in my carry-on. When Jeff and Stella came home around four a.m., because the hotel they were at was too noisy, he woke me up. I realized I was about to miss my flight. I finished packing and headed out the door and hugged him. He hugged me back. "You don't have to go," he whispered. And it was tempting to stay. Very tempting. To just crawl back into bed with him and Stella. But I took one look at that linen closet and knew I could have no more part in this. I mean, it was other stuff, too, but the bastardization of our linen closet was not insignificant.

It wasn't always easy living with Jeff. And hey, it's not all roses living with me, either, or so I'm told.

I HAVE ALWAYS BEEN THE BAD ROOMMATE. It's not something I'm proud of. I am trying to heal from Bad Roommate Syndrome. And step one in my recovery is to acknowledge and take responsibility for all the indiscretions in my past. So, now, for all those who wish to read—and especially to anyone thinking about living with me in the future—here is my full accounting of all the sins I have committed and apologies for the same, listed in chronological order by roommate.

ROOMMATE #1: Wendy, freshman year, college

Wendy is and was a gem of a human being. I'm not sure I've met a Wendy before and I don't think I've met one since. She's the one my dad still asks about. Freshman year. University of Maryland. Easton 5. She was from Newton, Massachusetts, I was from Rockville, Maryland. She was white and skinny and I was non-white and non-skinny. We were each other's first roommates and I was gonna be the best roommate in the world. Sadly, it was hardly so.

Wendy, here are my apologies:

- I'm sorry I liked eating Cocoa Puffs with warm milk but I never knew what to do with the leftover milk so I would just put the bowl of milk in the fridge until the entire fridge was just bowls of chocolate milk.

- I'm sorry that whenever I went to the convenience store to get stuff for both of us I'd come back with a bag of mini marshmallows and one bottle of water, neither of which you asked for.

- I'm sorry for that time in our room when I was standing on my bed hanging laundry, wearing only a towel because I'd just gotten out of the shower, and you were on the phone with your boyfriend and I thought it would be fun to open my towel and secretly expose myself behind your back. Had I known that your boyfriend would ask, "What's Sarah up to?" at that very moment, causing you to turn around and see me gyrating my naked tits wildly, I would not have done this. Okay, I probably would not have done this.

- I'm sorry I'd get down on my knees and pray to God every night before bed. It was a habit I picked up in high school. I almost felt like it was bad luck if I didn't. Which must've been weird to see, given my naked gyrating behind your back and the parade of men I brought into our room that year.

- I'm sorry my alarm clock played "Connection" by Elastica every morning at six a.m. at full volume and I overslept every day, forcing you to get out of bed and walk over to my nightstand to turn it off. (Go listen to the first 30 seconds of this song and tell me you would not have killed me.)

- I'm sorry for being jealous of how much attention your side of the room got with your family pictures and so I put up this huge collage above my bed with all this basic shit I got at Spencer's Gifts just to compete with you. If it's any consolation, no one gave a fuck about my collage, and I spent a lot of money and an entire weekend on it.

- I'm sorry that I was annoyed that everyone wanted to watch *Friends* and *The X-Files* on my TV because I didn't like people coming into our room and not paying attention to me and, much worse, paying attention to two shows I hated at the time, but only because they got more attention than me.

- I'm sorry I was jealous of how guys would look at you when we were walking around campus, and I'd strain my neck leaning into your face so I could convince myself they were staring at me, too.

- I'm sorry I always wanted attention but I never wanted to admit I wanted attention, so when we were speaking in a group and no one had paid attention to me yet, I'd say in a deep voice out of the corner of my mouth, "So, SARAH, how was YOUR day?"

- I'm sorry for that time I discovered Zima and vodka in the same night and went to a frat party and told a guy he didn't have a forehead, he had a fivehead, and walked away, leaving you to apologize.

- I'm sorry I then came back to our room and threw up in your trash can.

- I'm sorry you had to clean your trash can because I was too hungover to do it myself.

Thank you, Wendy, for always being fun, for keeping in touch, and for showing me what a good roommate looks like.

ROOMMATE #2: Abla, grad school

Abla is and was a gem of a human being. I definitely haven't met an Abla before and I haven't met one since. She's the other one my dad still asks about. When I got into Georgia Tech for grad school, I found out about an open room in the house Abla was renting near campus. I don't even know if I met her before I moved in. She had a cat named Spencer, named after Lady Di, and I was allergic to cats but figured I'd be okay. I was far from okay. I mean, the cat didn't bother me, but I was a bad roommate.

Abla, here are my apologies:

- I'm sorry I kept leaving plates of tuna fish on the counter so Spencer would lick them, and in the process of licking them, push them onto the floor, shattering them.

- I'm sorry that every day I would dump so much sugar in my peppermint tea that you felt compelled to introduce me to the concept of sugar cubes so I could control my sugar intake. Or so that I would stop finishing off your sugar. Either way, I appreciate it.

- I'm sorry that I never really got along with your cat. Spencer was often just trying to be friends with me, but I saw him as a nuisance, especially since I couldn't pet him due to my allergies.

- I'm sorry I never really appreciated the art project that you hung in the dining room. I still don't know what it was, but I think you explained it to me like 18 times.

- I'm sorry I always felt so dejected around my birthday that I made you celebrate it for the entire week.

- I'm sorry about my obsession with curly fries, forcing you to drive us to that same hole-in-the-wall place every Friday just so I could get them.

- I'm sorry I used you as unpaid labor for my thesis project "Reliving Last Night," an interactive movie I filmed in the living room one weekend, but it turned out I was filming when I thought I wasn't and I wasn't filming when I thought I was, which meant we had to do it all over again the following weekend.

- I'm sorry I had my boyfriend move in with us, creating a very awkward not-quite *Three's Company* situation where you pretty much felt trapped in your bedroom the whole time because he and I had taken over the whole rest of the apartment and we weren't even polite about it.

- I'm sorry my boyfriend used to dip tobacco and leave his tobacco spit in containers of soda everywhere.

- I'm sorry for all the unnecessarily loud fake orgasms.

Thank you, Abla. For your endless kindness and understanding.

ROOMMATE #3: Sarah, East Village, met on Craigslist

Sarah is and was a gem of a human being. I have met a million Sarahs before and will likely meet a million more. She's the one my dad never asks about because they never met. I found Sarah through Craigslist when I moved to New York for the summer to attend the Stella Adler Summer Conservatory. And I knew we'd get along when soon after our "interview," we were watching *The Bachelor* and making very interesting predictions on who would win. I was probably the best roommate to Sarah, since I'd already had so much practice, but there are still some places I went wrong.

Sarah, here are my apologies:

- I'm sorry for eating all your food constantly and trying desperately to replace it before you noticed and always failing pretty miserably.

- I'm sorry for never buying groceries.

- I'm sorry for not being able to protect you from that douchebag who you thought you were in love with because I was too obsessed with my own douchebag I thought I was in love with.

- I'm sorry for that time I decided to shave my entire body in the shower and I didn't clean it up and when you called me on it I pretended like that wasn't my hair despite the fact that *no one else lives here and you're blond.*

- I'm sorry for constantly begging you to come to my stand-up and improv shows.

- I'm sorry for hating your yellow couch but being too scared to tell you that I wanted a new couch so I had to get my other friend to tell you.

- I'm sorry for telling you your brother could sleep in my bedroom because I was off to Spain but then I forgot my passport so I missed my flight and needed my bedroom back.

- I'm sorry for never telling you how much it meant to me, on the day I had my Google interview, walking out to see a handmade "Good luck, Sarah!" sign outside my bedroom door.

- I'm sorry that when "we" threw parties, you made all the food and I did nothing. Well, I guess I . . . nope. I did nothing.

- I'm sorry for moving out abruptly to go live with my boyfriend, leaving you without a couch and with a month to find a new roommate. But to be fair, that boyfriend later became my husband, who later became my ex-husband.

- I'm sorry for being mad that you wouldn't come to my wedding because you'd just been to four weddings as a single woman and didn't want to do it again, which seemed like an excuse at the time but now that I'm single again I see how valid that is.

Thank you, Sarah, for being a friend and a confidant and a great person to watch *The Bachelor* with.

LIVING WITH JEFF WAS ANOTHER STORY. Spouses are so much more codependent than roommates.

I always felt like I had to go to bed when he went to bed even when I wasn't tired. Which led to a lot of scrolling in bed from about 11 p.m. to two a.m., while pretending to sleep. Which was silly, because I'm a night person. And he's a morning person. Truly, if we'd have just gotten to the point where we understood we had different schedules, we might still be married today.

When he started working from home during the pandemic, I really resented how he actually *worked*. I'd been working from home for five years at that point, so I understood what working from home meant. But when my husband started doing it, he really didn't. He would get up at six a.m. every morning, work out, take a shower, get fully dressed (top AND bottom), make breakfast, and then go into his office, sit at his desk, and, get this, actually work. Like, all day.

I was like, dude, you are doing this all wrong. You are supposed to wake up at six a.m. and think this is going to be the most productive day of your life, then go back to bed until 10. Then you wake up, you go to the kitchen in your pajamas and eat literally everything until like noon, then it's time to go back to sleep. Then around two p.m., you wake up again, answer one email, and then it's time to get high. That's how working from home works. So did the pandemic affect our relationship? Yeah, I mean, my husband made me feel super unproductive.

And when I discovered weed around 2019, that was tough, too. He didn't like when I was high. But I loved it. So then I started getting high secretively. He'd say he could tell when I was high and when I was not high, and I was like, *when am I not high?*

And of course there was the reality television. When we first got married it was all we watched. Monday night: *Below Deck Mediterranean*. Tuesdays: *90 Day Fiancé*. Wednesdays: *Married at First Sight*. Thursdays were rough, but Fridays we had *Celebrity Rehab*. And Saturday mornings we stayed in bed watching *Cheaters*. I have not watched a single episode of any of these programs since we got divorced. Maybe he hasn't, either. Do these shows just exist to convince married couples that their lives could be worse, thereby willing them to stay together longer than they should? Tom Brokaw really needs to look into it.

We'd developed these little weekly rituals that we had trouble changing even when they weren't working for us. In San Francisco, every Saturday we'd drive to this Vietnamese place for banh mi and summer rolls. But it was a 20-minute drive, followed by 30 minutes trying to find a parking spot for a 15-minute meal, and then it would somehow take two hours to get home. But if we didn't do that, what else were we going to do?

And I guess we ran so far out of things to do that now we were doing the only thing we hadn't done yet: getting a divorce.

The plan was for us to both move out of the apartment and find other apartments. We had already given our notice that we were breaking the lease. Our apartment was listed on StreetEasy. They were going to start showing it.

In July, I still hadn't found a place to live, but Jeff had. He signed a lease and put down a deposit and had a move-in date and I cried. I mourned our relationship, I mourned the future we were supposed to have, I mourned and mourned and mourned. For about an hour. And then I asked him the question that had been baking in my mind ever since the night I hid weed gummies inside Blow Pop wrappers for my flight to Florida. I asked if it was okay if I moved back into our apartment by myself. AND HE SAID YES. He said yes! Wow, is this how men feel when they propose?

The day I came back to that apartment was pure joy. I walked through my fancy lobby, and into my elevator, and into the cool, recycled air of my hermetically sealed apartment as a single woman, for the first time in over a decade, and the only thing I wanted to do was drop off my bags at the door and run around screaming, "MINE! MINE! IT'S ALL MINE!!!!"

When I got to the bedroom, I opened the linen closet and there it was . . . NOTHING. There was NOTHING in the linen closet.

I folded a sheet and placed it delicately on the center shelf. I stared at it. I kneeled before it. I raised my arms. And I shouted, "IN THE NAME OF THE QUEEN!"

Sheets.

Periwinkle Can Go Fuck Itself:
My Life in Colors

ALWAYS THOUGHT IT was stupid to ask someone, "What's your favorite color?" But as I've gotten older and taken more edibles, I realize this is actually a very interesting question. It's especially helpful if you've just gotten out of a codependent relationship where your partner made all the decorating decisions and you don't even know what your vibe is. If you're someone who's lived your entire life as a people pleaser and assimilated your personality into oblivion, figuring out how you feel about colors is a great place to start. I sure did.

BLACK

Almost every item of clothing I own is black. My purse is black. My iPhone case is black. My soul is—probably black. I love a pitch-black sky; you feel so small. I love black humor. There's not a single other color black doesn't look good with. It's so simple. It doesn't demand anything. It can be something you don't even notice. Or it can be so eye-catching, like a black smoky eye. Have you seen those cars with matte black finishes? So sexy. I got matte black nails once, also sexy. I will go to bat for black any day of the week. Including Black Friday, which is actually the only black thing I don't really care for.

BLUE

For most of my life, if you asked me what my favorite color was, I'd say blue. It was only after my divorce, when I started to do some real soul-searching, that I realized I hate most blues.

Navy blue is boring as hell. No offense to the Navy, or to the guy who was wearing a navy-blue sweater when I said I hated navy blue and then backtracked and said, "I like it on you, though!" I have a navy-blue couch and I hate it. I wish my navy-blue couch knew how disappointed I am in it every time I see it. But I'll never get a new couch. I'm so lazy.

You know what else is lazy? Periwinkle. The only thing I like about periwinkle is the word "periwinkle." It's got such a fun name for such a dull color. Four syllables for a color that'll put you to sleep instantly. Periwinkle tries too hard to please everyone, and you just hate it because it reminds you of yourself. In my twenties, my wingman Alex was trying to figure out what kind of guys I liked. When I pointed out a few who I thought were hot, he noticed they all had one thing in common: a Lands' End periwinkle button-down shirt. In other words, the most generic men I could find. Periwinkle will never challenge the status quo. Periwinkle IS the status quo.

There's only one blue that is truly beautiful, truly worth its weight in gold (a color I'll address later). And that's teal.

Teal is superious. Teal reminds me of the ocean at my favorite beach, Doctor's Cave in Montego Bay, Jamaica. Any mixture of blue and green takes me to that beach and the beef patty and cocoa bread and ginger beer I'd enjoy on the sand. Unlike periwinkle, teal is not lazy. It is working overtime in the subtlest of ways. You can't even tell if it's one syllable or two. Is it "teel"? Or "teee-aalll"? Teal is blue and green. Teal is a blue that knew it wasn't enough so it brought green on and they made each other better. Perfect harmony. I love you, teal. Never change.

BEIGE

Baayyyyjjjj. Beige is aggressively boring. But so seductive. Seductive in its boringness and unobtrusiveness. It says pick me, you won't even know I'm here. I'm the absence of nothing. I make no statements. I mean, it's khaki, it's paint, it's my skin tone. Except on my skin it's very confusing—my beige skin is the reason no one knows what I am. My skin is the color of an Amazon package, and like Amazon packages, people want to know what's in there, where I came from, how long I've been sitting here. Mom LOVES beige. Every shade of beige is hers. My mom has a color wheel from Benjamin Moore and she just looks at beiges all day long. Other colors, too, but mainly the beiges. Currently the dining room, kitchen, and living room are all three slightly different shades of beige. Sometimes she'll hold up one beige next to another beige and ask me which beige I like better. I never know what to tell her.

GRAY

Gray is one of those colors I love one second and hate the next. Barely gray walls, beautiful. Dark gray walls, awful. You can never find the right shade of gray, have you ever noticed that? It's always slightly too light or slightly too dark. The only gray that's sometimes appealing is silver. Like the color of aluminum. Metal. The color of my MacBook. Space gray they call it. But these gray hairs on my head can all go to hell. I color them and five minutes later they're back. They are relentless.

RAINBOW

Rainbow's okay, I guess. Sometimes I feel like it's trying too hard to cheer me up, you know? It's like, just let me be sad, rainbow.

WHITE

I fucking love white. Not in any kind of supremacy sense, obviously. But mostly when there's something up against the white that makes the white look more white, you know? Like black text on a white page. Although I think there'd be something pleasing about being in an all-white room, where you can't see where it begins or ends, like in *The Matrix*. I wore an off-white dress at my wedding. I was 36. I have a white sofa. I love it but it's taken me a while to relax around it. My mother refuses to sit on it because she's scared to ruin it. I almost want to purposefully mess it up so she'll see it's already ruined and sit on it. I love white sheets. But only because if there's a bug you can see it easily. But trying to put a white duvet cover on a white comforter is damn near impossible, especially if you're high. I got stuck inside a duvet for an hour once. I love white space. I appreciate a little white noise, although absolute silence is the best. White is a color that sounds like it's questioning itself, you know? Whyyyyy-tuh? I appreciate the introspection.

RED

I'm not a fan of red. I don't think I own anything red except a dress I'm giving away and a sweater and another sweater and some lingerie. Too flashy, you know? Too arresting. The color of blood. The color of stop. Red is anxiety. Red is car crashes and sirens. There's that song, "The Lady in Red." I've always hated it.

I believe every woman goes through a fuchsia phase. Fuchsia bike shorts, fuchsia tank top, fuchsia lipstick, fuchsia blush. Fuchsia fuchsia fuchsia. But then you grow out of it. And you look at fuchsia like, relax, fuchsia, relax.

Maroon and burgundy are some truly gross colors. Maroon 5: not bad, Ron Burgundy: great, but maroon and burgundy are just so heavy. They weigh me down.

GREEN

For the longest time I didn't think I liked green. I had no appreciation for it. I never noticed it, and when I did, I thought to myself, *Ugh, green.* But when I woke up after my divorce I realized how much I loved green. The color of trees. The color of grass. The color of the plants in my mom's garden, all shades of green. The color of jealousy, which I feel for anyone who's accomplished anything I haven't been able to yet. The color of money, which I wish I didn't worry about so much and yet gives me so much freedom and power. The color of the Starbucks logo, a company I've given so much of my freedom and power to. All in all, green is a prominent force in my life. Also, you can't have teal without green, so there's that. Green means go. But it's a specific kind of go, it's the go you get when you're waiting to go. Not like an angry get up and go now, but more like an okay, your time is now. You can't say green without smiling a little bit. And that's how I feel about green, finally, after all these years. It makes me smile.

When I first moved to New York, I tried to break out of my black, white, gray, beige addiction and bought sweet-pea-green curtains. I really liked them at first. Really, really liked them. Then I hated them. I fucking hated them. Why, why did I try to step out of my comfort zone? I think the reason I thought I'd like those sweet-pea-green curtains was that I once used that color on a button for some ad campaign when I was working at IQTV and I fell in love with it. And looking back, I do love that color. I saw a sweet-pea green convertible Porsche once. It was so cute.

Hands down the best green is neon, peridot, or citron. I love this color. It's a shot of adrenaline. It's the color of my Ivy Park sneakers, my Ann Taylor Loft sweater, and my midcentury modern dining room chairs. There is no ignoring this color, but it is not needy. It knows it's the shit. You don't simply like this color. You succumb to it. Word of peridot caution, though: Do not attempt to use this color as a French manicure tip because it will look like you dipped your hands in urine.

GOLD

In my mind there's been a long-simmering debate between gold, silver, platinum, chrome, pewter, polished nickel, and rubbed bronze.

For jewelry, for furniture, for cabinet knobs and faucets and other appliances. And it's taken me a long time to admit it after being bullied out of it, but goddammit I love gold. Not for appliances. Or faucets. But jewelry, yes. I think I'd have more gold jewelry if I hadn't been told over and over again that gold is lame. And I'd have more gold-accented furniture if that was the case, too. But then I get gold-accented furniture and all I hear are the voices in my head saying how cheesy it looks. Maybe it's just the 1960s thing. I love the 1960s and the gold of it all. The unabashed love of gold. Before people decided silver and platinum were cooler. Then they came out with white gold. As if we can even tell the difference between white gold and silver. White gold makes no sense. White chocolate makes no sense. The only thing that makes sense is "White Christmas," but that's over because of climate change. Which I do care about. Unlike Trump. So don't think I'm just like him because I like gold.

PURPLE

I was convinced of purple's greatness for much of my early childhood. It felt rebellious. It felt weird. It was different. It didn't make sense. It was pink but it was blue, it was the color of the sky sometimes, and sometimes not. It could be deep, it could be shallow. It could be feminine like lavender and smell delicious, but it could be masculine like *Purple Rain*, the album by Prince, who also seemed into purple but maybe just because it also started with the letter P, I don't know much about Prince. I saw Prince in concert twice and he never played "Kiss." God, I love that confidence. That's what purple is, you didn't ask for it because you didn't even know it existed but then you get it and you're like, huh, I didn't know that was an option but it's kind of cool. I have to admit now, though, that purple seems pretty childish and myopic. It seems frivolous to choose anything purple in this economy. Purple was Yahoo!'s logo color, which I feel is still one of the reasons why that company ultimately failed. I mean, that purple could not be taken seriously, by anyone. It was the color of Barney the dinosaur.

YELLOW

I really don't like yellow. Yellow is the color of the sun, which shines in my eyes every morning because I sleep with the shades up because I like to look at the night sky, but then the sun comes up and ruins it all. I'd much prefer to be bathed in white light than yellow light. I hate when you buy a bulb and you think it's going to be white and it's yellow. I was obsessed with that song "Yellow" by Coldplay for a long time. But other than that, I try to avoid it.

LEOPARD PRINT

I had this great leopard-print sweaterdress I got at Express because in my early thirties I only shopped at Express. And I was dating this guy, Roderick. Rod-er-ick. No nickname. Every time I said his name, I had to say the whole fucking thing. He was the type of guy who walked around with a big book he hasn't read. The type of insecure man who demanded I think all his ideas were brilliant. And if I didn't, he'd go find evidence that they were brilliant so he could prove me wrong. I was obviously in love with him and dutifully applauded all his ideas, and when he needed to borrow $300 I loaned it to him without a thought.

I met Roderick on Match.com, and after about a month of dating he asked me to be his girlfriend, and I was flattered and said yes and thought I was going to marry him because he was tall and handsome and from Barbados and I'm from Jamaica and isn't that perfect? Roderick was always super excited to go down on me, but then he'd come back up after a few minutes like he accomplished something. And I'd always make him think he did, because I guess that felt just as good as AN ORGASM, SARAH? I missed him so much when I went home to visit my family and I was surprised to see him show up—not at my parents' house but on Match.com, where it said he'd been active in the last 24 hours. And then it said he was active right at that very minute. And I thought, *That's weird, why's he on Match.com when we are in a committed exclusive relationship and also why does Match.com have this stupid fucking feature?* Of course, hard to ask your boyfriend why he's on Match when the only reason you know he's on Match is because you were on Match but you were only on Match to turn off your Match. I called him on it anyway. I asked what he was doing on Match. And he said he got an email about a message he got from someone else and he was reading it. Okay. Cool.

I came back from my parents' house with an ear infection and I couldn't hear very well but was too scared to say I couldn't hear his dumb ideas, so I was just nodding and smiling, and he was like, can you even hear me, and I said no, not really, and he was like why are you pretending like you can, then? As if that's not what all women do to him all the time. He got this idea for a tourist website for Barbados so I got the domain BarbadosGetaways.com and started to design it, until he then decided a website to track champion horses would be better so then I got ChampionHorseTracker.com and started to design that. I had a full-time job at Google.

Then my birthday came around. And I know this guy is broke, so I'm not expecting much. But what I got was less than that. In the morning I was greeted by a Blue Mountain E-CARD. An E-CARD. That didn't even have a message in it. It didn't even say "Love, Roderick." It just said "—Roderick." Then. Then the bastard came over to my place. And I thought for sure. For sure he'd have something for me. It was my birthday! We'd been dating for two months. And do you know what he had? A book. For himself. To fake-read on the train. We talked for a while on my bed and then he said he was hungry, and he was going to go get something to eat and he'd come back. And I thought, *Okay, now he's going to get me something.* Like a flower, a cupcake, a raspberry, for chrissakes. But no, he came back with a slice of pizza. One slice of pizza. For himself. Which he ate.

In front of me. On my birthday. And I started crying. Because I was really fucking hurt. And do you know what he did? He broke up with me and left. He left me crying on my birthday. And I was so heartbroken. I was sad. Over *that guy*.

I eventually got over Roderick. But one thing I never got over is that leopard-print dress. He invited me to an off-off-off-Broadway show, and when he invited me he definitely left off several offs. He got the tickets on Groupon, and we had to unfold our own chairs. And I wore my leopard-print dress because I wanted to look sexy for him, but when I showed up he seemed distressed. He wouldn't look me in the eye. And I didn't know what was wrong but I kept asking as we were eating the store-bought cookies and lemonade they served as refreshments in the kitchenette next to the stage.

Finally, as we were seated and the lights were coming down and the play was just about to start, he leaned over and whispered, "I really don't like your dress." And then I got to sit there for an hour and a half and think about that while I watched a play about capitalism or something. And after that play I told him to fuck right off. Just kidding, I went home and I burned the dress in the fireplace. I burned it. Because I said, If Roderick doesn't like this, then I can never wear it again. And now whenever I see any kind of animal print I think of him.

And I fucking buy it.

ORANGE

Orange is fine.

Thank God for My
Broken Uterus

I'VE ALWAYS WANTED A BABY. Ever since it seemed like that would fix my marriage, I really wanted one. Yeah. A baby would fix things, I thought. Having a baby would be fun. Jeff would be excited. I'd be excited. Everyone would be like, Wow! Congratulations! When are you due? We'd share pictures of my bump on Instagram and get so many likes. My mom would come to stay with us to take care of the baby. Maybe Jeff's mom would want to come, too? We don't have room for that . . . Maybe they won't come at all . . . Maybe it'll just be me and Jeff taking care of a baby . . .

We had just gotten married, and moved across the country to San Francisco, and bought a home, and a ficus, and so a kid was the next logical thing. But we were only sort of half trying to have a kid. Like, the bottom halves of us were trying, but the top halves were like, *whatever, if we have a kid, great, if we don't, no big deal* (because if there's anything you want to be 50/50 on, it's having a child). So one day I took a test, and I was pregnant! And we were excited for about two days. Then we started thinking nine months ahead and it got stressful fast. We started discussing daycare and schools and very soon I did not want a baby. Jeff and I were not good at accomplishing tasks together. We had to retile the bathroom once. I still haven't recovered.

I told Jeff we maybe weren't ready for a child. He was fine with whatever I wanted to do. We planned to go to Planned Parenthood, even though we were in San Francisco at the time and probably could have just gone to CVS.

Right before we left, I looked up some pictures of zygotes. I was doing anything to talk myself out of it. But my mind was made up. We went to Planned Parenthood and that was my first time ever going there. I'd always supported Planned Parenthood, even as a teenager. I didn't even need to read their mission; the title said it all to me. In my youth I believed vasectomies should be mandatory for all men until they were older and able to pass some sort of online quiz. Anyway, my first and only visit to Planned Parenthood was very heartening. It was everything I thought it would be: helpful, safe, comforting. They did an ultrasound and, at first, they said it was twins. Which gave me pause. I wondered if they had some sort of buy one, get one deal. If I'd need a coupon. But then they looked closer and realized it wasn't a viable pregnancy. I was going to have a miscarriage. I was trying to get an abortion and God said, *No worries, I got this one*. Or maybe the fetus heard Google Maps say, "Navigating to Planned Parenthood," and it was like, *Fuck this bitch, she can't fire me, I quit*.

They told me to get an appointment with my regular gyno. Jeff and I headed home. I told him that at first they said it was twins. His response was, "Oh, wow, we could have started a band." That's when I knew God made the right decision. Since we knew they'd tell us we were having a miscarriage, Jeff and I showed up for that appointment with balloons and a mom-to-be shirt and a big bag of toys, just to make it extra awkward. Just kidding, we didn't do that, but we thought about it. They scheduled a D&C, which I playfully dubbed an AC/DC. A few weeks later, I got my AC/DC and it was awful and I threw up out of the Lyft on the way home and it was over. The strangest part was visiting friends of ours that very same week and them telling us they were pregnant with their first child. It felt too callous to go, *Oh my god that's crazy we just had an AC/DC!* Jeff and I just gave each other a little look and congratulated them.

I never really wanted to be a mother. I don't know how to take care of anything. People have always taken care of me. Once I told Katie I'd like to be the "mom" of our friend group and make sure to have snacks for everyone and she was completely supportive, but literally every time she asks me if I have snacks, I never do. And she's a good friend so she stopped asking. I don't like being the adult. I never have. I never will.

How could I have ever been a mom when I lost custody of my own dog? I never had treats. I never had poop bags, I never had toys, I never had anything. Losing custody of my dog gets harder every year. I was kind of loving my freedom at first, I didn't feel as tied down, but now I miss that little girl. We worked so hard to get a dog, too. We'd go to the SPCA every weekend but didn't connect with any of the dogs there. We applied for dogs online, but the application process was so rigorous. I had to ask my friends to write recommendations. We had to do a home inspection, write an essay, do a video interview. And by the time we did all that, the dog we wanted was gone. At one point, Jeff and I said fuck it, it'd be easier to have a kid. But I didn't want to be pushing a baby around in a stroller and have people whisper behind my back: *You know why she has that baby? She couldn't get approved for a dog.*

The truth is, before Jeff and I got married, before there was a situation that needed fixing, I knew I didn't want kids. I knew as soon as I had a child, I wouldn't be able to stop thinking about that child even when I wanted to think about something else, even for a split second, I wouldn't be able to. It would be exactly how I was with wedding planning. When I was planning our wedding, I did NOT want to be thinking about wedding planning every second, but I couldn't help it. It occupied every spare thought in my mind:

- The little details and decisions drove me crazy the most.
- Multitasking was impossible.
- Context switching between planning the wedding and doing anything else was impossible.

- No matter how hard I tried to wake up and write or do anything creative before I answered emails about the wedding, or filled out spreadsheets, or looked at my to-do list—it never happened.

- What happened instead was me chipping away at this beast of a wedding plan.

- Which, to be fair, wasn't even really a beast. We only had 55 guests.

- But it still felt like so much work.

- And I was so stressed.

- I was stressed about my wedding. The day that's supposed to be the happiest day of my life and I found myself thinking over and over again, *I can't wait for it to be over.*

- How awful is that?

- Well, it's not *too* awful.

- Planning my wedding just wasn't my thing.

- But for a lot of people, it *is* their thing. In fact, their entire existence revolves around their wedding day.

- So yeah, in some respects, it's good that wedding planning is not "my thing."

- I wanted to marry Jeff, but planning the wedding made me lose sight of what was really important.

- I also got mad at pretty much everyone in my life, including Jeff, because I felt alone, like I was doing it on my own, and like no one was taking it as seriously or treating it as importantly as I was.

- And I'm pretty sure this is how I would have been with a baby.

- You have this thing that requires constant attention.

- You try to just "take care of it" and move on to something else—but you never can.

- You try to be excited about it and for brief moments you are, but for most of the time it's a burden.

- It's a burden on your mind, your time, and your wallet.

- Listen, I'm sure a baby would bring me more joy than completing a wedding planning spreadsheet or dissecting a bill for flowers.

- But taking care of it, prioritizing it in my life, having to figure out the logistics of its care, making decisions about what to do with it all the time, in case of this, in case of that, when this happens—ugh. No.

- So it was a good lesson, this wedding-planning business. A lesson in how much I did not want a baby.

- There are just too many other things I'd rather do.

I REALLY DON'T LIKE being considered an adult in my family at all. What happened to my washbelly status? It's all gone. I remember the exact moment I realized it was gone.

I was visiting my brother and his family in Maryland for the weekend. He and his wife, Susie, went off to a party and left me alone with my nephews, who were 12 and 17, my nephew's girl-friend, also 17, and Susie's mother, who's 75. And of course, my dumbass decides to take an edible, and everyone's hungry and looking at me like I'm supposed to do something about it.

Then it hits me—I AM supposed to do something about it. I'm the adult here. Wait, I'm the adult? Dinner is MY job? I'm in CHARGE? But I'm the WASHBELLY. And I'm HIGH.*

I spring into panicked action, which is a very Sarah Cooper thing to do, and ask if they wanted to order something. Here's my phone, here's DoorDash, here's Postmates, here's Uber Eats, order whatever you want. Yeah. I would've been a great mom. My nephews start arguing over delivery fees. This is when I learn that they choose restaurants by how much the delivery fee is. My nephews are already better at money than I am. They decide on Chick-fil-A because the delivery fee is 99 cents. And it takes everyone literally YEARS to place their orders. When I'm high, time goes very, very slowly. Then the food comes. And I'm—lost. I tell you I'm lost. I'm setting the dinner table, shaking, worried everyone won't want to sit and eat together. And it was gonna break my heart. I would've felt like a failure. A complete and utter aunt failure.

At our next session, my therapist would say, "Why would them not sitting together for dinner be your fault? Them not wanting to sit at the dinner table is not a reflection of you." And during that session I got a glimpse of what my therapy sessions would've been like if I'd had kids.

I am so terrified no one will want to eat with me that I set the table, then I go hide in the bathroom like a psychopath. I can't bear the feeling of sitting at the table WAITING for my nephews and the girlfriend and their grandma to sit with me. If I'd been a mom, that would've been the title of my memoir: *Hiding in the Bathroom.*

At some point I hear them all sitting down at the table, and I emerge from the bathroom. And Tyler wants to take his food into his room, and I say, Come on, let's eat together. And we sit together. But Ryan turns on the TV. Do I tell him to turn it off? No,

---

* Note here for George and Susie, I wasn't really high, it's just better for the story. I swear. I promise.

because he's not really watching it. We're talking. And it's not too bad. I feel kind of like a success. But I'm kind of tense the whole time, wanting to keep them interested enough to sit at the table. I'm trying way too hard to keep them entertained so they'll stay at the dinner table and my feelings won't be hurt. Fifteen minutes later they all get up to leave and it kinda breaks my heart, but we got like 15 minutes together, so that's something, right? It is something, I tell myself.

If I'd been a parent, I would've been dead of a heart attack by age 45 with the level of stress caused by orchestrating one dinner from Chick-fil-A delivery.

WE HAD ANOTHER MISCARRIAGE four years after the first one. Like I said, I'm not good with segues. This time we were planning to keep it. But when we went in to listen to the heartbeat, there wasn't one. And I spent the next several months feeling broken, like there was something my body was supposed to be able to do and it couldn't do it. What a disappointment. How un-Jamaican and un-perfectionist of me.

And yet, I can't tell you how happy I am that I did not have either of those babies.

Society believes every woman wants a baby. Even the ones who don't want a baby still get their eggs frozen *just in case* they want a baby. Get married, well, you must want a baby. Oh my god, you two would have the cutest babies! People would say, You want *kids*, don't you? *You* want kids, don't you? Usually as they were pushing their own kids toward me. But, ladies, you do get to an age when people stop asking you if you want kids. All my life I've been asked if I want kids but now I'll be hanging out with my girlfriends and someone will go, "Sophie, do you want another kid? Are you going to give Mark a little brother or sister? Angela, do you want kids? Are you guys gonna have kids? Sarah . . . uh, you could adopt? How's that comedy thing going, is that working out?"

I thank God every day for my broken uterus.[*] I mean, I wanted an abortion the first time. But the second one I would have had. Because by then, the situation really needed fixing.

When I think about the life I'd have now if I'd had kids, it makes me nauseous with psychosomatic morning sickness. I sometimes think about how close I came to that life, in a relationship with someone who wasn't right for me, with children who needed me. I imagine I'd be too exhausted to create or write and I'd feel like shit about it every day. Not saying I would've died inside, but I'd probably feel dead inside. It's like that scene in *Muriel's Wedding* where the mom is just standing in the kitchen staring into space doing nothing other than waiting for an order from her husband or children. That part stuck with me. People who are *there* but not quite *there* just from having their feelings trampled or ignored so much that they just decided it was easier to stop having them.

If it weren't for my best friend, Katie, and the therapist she introduced me to, and the vibrator she gave me, and ALL OF YOU sharing my videos so I could support myself and get my own health insurance, it would have been very hard for me to leave, and with a kid it would have felt impossible. And for those of you who have gotten out of a situation like that, I know it was hard. But you never know who you're inspiring by living a life that's true to you. Like, Katie left her unhealthy relationship, which was literally the only way I was able to leave my unhealthy relationship. Plus, you know, a bit of an assist from God on the whole broken uterus thing.

Thanks, God. I owe you one. Or two.

---

[*] I do not know for sure if my uterus is broken, it just sounded funnier than "reproductive issues." Also, if you actually have a broken uterus and you wish it wasn't broken, I apologize if this makes you feel sad. Sometimes I wish mine wasn't broken and I could go back in time and marry that guy from college and learn what it's like to be pregnant and what it feels like to have another human call me "Mommy" because I'm literally their mommy and not because some guy at work thinks I'm being bossy.

Red Flags You're Dating a Robot

'VE BEEN DIVORCED FOR TWO YEARS NOW and I don't know if I ever want to fall in love again. I don't know if I ever want to dedicate that much of myself to a man ever again. Especially because most of them are robots. They're not even real human beings. They're robots. Just running scripts over and over again. They're technology. And I know you think I'm making a metaphor here, but I'm not. Many men are, quite literally, robots. Built by Elon Musk with bits and bytes, ones and zeros, and programmed to populate the world with little half-human, half-robot androids to build his Teslas. Let's get into the science.

Now, what I'm about to say to you is going to make it sound like I'm Pee-wee Herman in *Pee-wee's Big Adventure* during that basement scene where he's losing his mind, but trust me, you could be dating a robot. Here are the signs:

1. **Tall with a good head of hair**

   When building these machines, Elon knew that height and hair will get most women to overlook just about anything, especially the fact that this is a robot.

2. **Monotonous voice**

   If your date uses the same tone of voice to say, "I went to Duke," as he does to say, "I'm gonna come," he's probably a robot. See, technology hasn't yet developed the, uhm, technology to make these kinds of tonal distinctions.

Which makes it extra ironic that, for centuries, women have been told to watch our various tones while these robots have been praised for having only *one* tone. But our many tones prove we're human. Their one tone proves they're robots.

3. **Works in your industry**

Elon knows that career-minded women love a power fuck. They love feeling like they're with someone great, and someone great usually means someone who's succeeded at something they're trying to do. So yeah, usually these robots are prime bait for us ambitious women, they lie in wait in our office buildings, at our coffee shops, and on our movie sets. They turn you on with how creative they are so they can suck you into a life of forgetting your dreams.

4. **Shuts down mentally after about an hour of conversation**

Most robots only have the AI language model for about an hour of realistic-seeming-but-wholly-simulated conversation. In addition, they won't have the capacity to remember any details from previous conversations. I contend that if we give these robots the capacity to remember previous details, that would probably take the conversation time down to 45 minutes or even 30, but it'd be worth it. Quality over quantity, I say. But engineers have studied women and realized we will put up with ALMOST ANYTHING as long as the guy is over six feet tall and has a good head of hair. In fact, women will think it's THEIR fault for being boring and they will go to their therapist and wonder what's going on with this guy because spending $200 an hour on therapy to analyze a FUCKING ROBOT is such a good use of your money, Sarah. And you'll put your own little therapist hat on and make up some story in your head about how his father was away a lot when he was a kid and so maybe he only got one hour at a time with his dad and maybe when his body reaches that hour point, he shuts the conversation down first, effectively rejecting me before I can reject him and sparing himself the pain of this childhood trauma. But no. No. No. No! He's a robot. It's a lack of processing power. That's it. That's all it is.

5. **Pretends to like Charlie Kaufman**

Robots have all been programmed to be "when in Rome" type people but only because it saves CPU. He'll often just go along with whatever's being said and adopt opinions from anyone around him. He'll even pretend to like Charlie Kaufman for you. Ha! You'll be so excited, like, *oh my god I met someone who loves Charlie Kaufman as much as I do,* but it'll all be a fucking ruse and it won't be until months later, when you mention *Being John Malkovich* and he's never heard of it, that you'll realize this robot was only pretending to like Charlie Kaufman so it would seem like you guys had some obscure thing in common and were meant to be together and maybe even have kids together even though you decided you didn't want kids, which is just how fucking dangerous these robots are.

6. **Lack of blinking**

Blinking can be affected by so many factors. It's a very delicate software, hardware, front-end, and back-end system. And because these robots don't actually need to moisten their eyes, the timing of their blinking will seem off or they'll forget to blink altogether. As a result, it will feel like this man is staring very intensely at you while sitting across from you at dinner. Very intensely. And it will make you think this guy is really, really interested in you. You'll feel beautiful. You'll feel special. You'll think he could be the one. But then you'll introduce him to your best friend, and he'll stare just as intensely at her. Right in front of you. With no regard for how you're feeling, no regard for the dagger in your heart every second he continues to stare at her. But it's very important you stay cool and make sure no one ever thinks anything bothers you, so you just sit there with a dead smile on your face, acting like a robot because you're dating a robot, but on the inside you are definitely not a robot. Which is unfortunate because that would be less painful. His staring at other women will have the added benefit of tethering you more closely to him because now you feel a jealousy that burns with the fire of a thousand suns, a very useful by-product of this blinking malfunction.

7. **Obsesses over the ratings and personal details of Lyft and Uber drivers**

Stick with me on this one. These robots aren't actually obsessed with the ratings and details of Lyft and Uber drivers, but they pretend to be because it makes them seem more human. Once assigned a driver, they will read their profile like it's *The New Yorker*, comment on the driver's name, their rating, their history, their hobbies. And you'll love that he treats those in our service industry with respect, and this will make you think you're falling in love with him, because that's the bar when you're a woman over 40. What's really going on here? Well, your robot boyfriend needs to interface with humans (i.e., Lyft and Uber drivers) in order to get the humans to do *what the technology wants them to do*. He will say, "Let's go to Soho House," and you'll be like yes, he really likes me, he's taking me to Soho House. But the truth is, his *iPhone* needed to go to Soho

House to download the latest sensory data to service its apps and it had nothing to do with how much he liked you. I have a feeling you didn't stick with me on that one.

8. **Sleeps with a fan**

I don't need to tell you how much robots overheat at night, so it's not surprising that they would sleep with a fan, or several fans, pointed at their bodies. The air cools them while the white noise neutralizes their operating systems so they can recharge their CPUs or motherboards or maybe upgrade to the latest software or what have you. It's very helpful for the robot, but it's awful for you because all these goddamn fans will render his room virtually inhospitable to human sleep. And you know this but you ignore it because you think sleeping over means the next step in this relationship so you'll pretend to be asleep when you're actually masturbating because HE DIDN'T MAKE YOU COME, AGAIN, and then you'll sit there lying awake, wanting to leave, wondering if you should sneak out or wake him up and you decide to wake him up so you tap him on the shoulder and you say you're gonna go and he goes through the normal robot progression of concern, then acceptance, then return to sleep state, so you get dressed and try to leave but the locks on his doors are confusing and you end up locking yourself in there and your Lyft is about to leave and now you're wondering if he's interfaced with your Lyft somehow to make sure you get charged a no-show fee and then you have to go wake him up again because you don't know how this door works, and then he tries to open it and it's stuck for him too and now you're picturing being trapped inside this tiny one-bedroom apartment with this robot for several days because he can't find a handyman and you're losing oxygen and you feel faint and just as you've accepted your new life as a robot prisoner he gets the door open and you breathe a sigh of relief.

9. **Doesn't have a type**

Most men have preferences. They like blondes, they like brunettes, they want someone Jewish, they like legs or butts or breasts, something. If they seem to just like it all? They're robots. They'll tell you they like all the things that you are—they'll say, "My previous girlfriends have all been older women, with curly hair and sexy lingerie, low maintenance, funny, cool, fun women like you." A simple Google search will prove that's not true, but you'll ignore it because he's over six feet tall and has a good head of hair. It's such a simple script, but it's so effective.

10. **Has a catchphrase but uses it wrong**

Five minutes into meeting you for the first time, after he's sat down and commented on your Moscow mule and commented on his glass of red wine and said a few other innocuous things, there's going to be a brief lull in the conversation and then he's going to say, "So what else is going on?"

Sorry, I just need to take a pause here because I need everyone to understand the gravity and the weight of a perfect stranger asking you, "What *else* is going on?"

What else is going on? You mean, besides everything about me, which you know nothing about because we just met? There's no part of this vague and ambivalent question that should appear five minutes into meeting someone. My brother sometimes asks me what else is going on. I might ask my mom or my sister that. Twenty minutes into the conversation. But not some guy I just met off Raya. What else is going on? I'm sitting here at this booth, I guess? I guess that's what else is going on. Seriously, you have nothing more specific to ask me?

I think it's the "else" that's throwing me off here. What's going on might be okay. What ELSE is going on. Like, I've already told you what's going on, now you want to know what ELSE is going on. Like you're already bored? But all you know about me is that my name is Sarah and I look like this and I'm drinking a Moscow mule. I just, I just, I just, I can't.

And this phrase will continue to haunt you, well into the sham of your relationship. It'll be cute when you point it out. And you think maybe he'll stop doing it. But he doesn't. He still says "What else is going on" five minutes into seeing you. You laugh about it and point it out again and he laughs, too, but he still does it. And when he meets your best friend, two minutes into that conversation he'll ask *her* what else is going on and you'll roll your eyes, embarrassed, and also a little jealous and also embarrassed of your jealousy.

My only guess is that, with this particular model, "so what else is going on" was mistakenly programmed by a sloppy engineer as the robot's key phrase to reset Wi-Fi when data collection is interrupted. The alternative is too bleak.

11. **Doesn't like emotions because he can't experience them himself**

Robots can't stand real humans. That's why they'll need you to start acting like a robot or it just won't work. See, there has to be a compromise when you're in a relationship with a robot. Either he has to learn how to have emotions or you need to lose yours, and since he can't learn any emotions, you'll need to lose yours. Now, he'll PRETEND to have emotions, and you'll respond to his programmed emotions with your real emotions until you realize you're just having the same conversation over and over and over again and you completely detach from your body and you become a dull shell of a human being, i.e., a robot.

12. Inability to multitask when his favorite show is on

Every robot is programmed to love one show, as if being into a TV show makes you human. But regardless, when *Succession* is on you won't be able to talk to him. He will not be able to look at you. It will be like you've turned into a mirage. I wonder if maybe his robot brain can't sense that it's a TV show he's watching, so he thinks Shiv and Roman are actually here with us right now. Or maybe he needs to capture an uninterrupted stream of data for a bootleg requested by the software engineers who built the robot and are watching the show through the robot's eyes. Either way, it's very frustrating and annoying and it makes you not want to watch TV with him, which is fine because being tethered to a robot to watch your shows is literally the lowest form of human being one can become.

13. Responds inappropriately to sweet text messages

Like, if you write, "I woke up thinking about you," he'll respond, "LOL." He'll apologize and say it was a mistake, but it was no mistake. Genuine emotion causes malfunctions. See, they are only programmed to respond to predictable behaviors and situations, so when you do something surprising and genuine, it will be impossible for them to know how to respond, so they'll cycle through and pick a response at random, and it often won't be the response you were looking for.

14. **Constantly argues with his therapist**

Sure, he has a therapist. Hell, he might have two therapists and a mentor. But it's all pointless. None of it's working. He spends his sessions arguing with one therapist, then pitting that therapist against the other therapist. He is simply not even remotely capable of gaining anything from therapy or mentorship, because he'll never change. He'll ask you about your therapy and explain why your therapist is full of shit, too. The robot's only goal here is to try to take down the therapy industry by convincing therapists that their job is worthless. This is a major goal of robots who want to take over our society. The more that humans understand ourselves, the less likely we are to succumb to our robot overlords. And the robots don't like this. So they sign up for therapy to drive therapists crazy, and these therapists eventually leave the business entirely, and it's one less person protecting us all from certain postapocalyptic Terminator-like destruction.

15. **Responds to new pieces of information with "Right"**

Doesn't matter what you tell him about yourself, no matter how deep down and personal a thing it is or even if it's a lie you're making up just to test him, he will always respond with the word "right." I was an orphan. Right. I got my period when I was 11. Right. My blood is green. Right.

16. **Love-bombing**

He'll make you think he's your boyfriend like, way too soon. He'll say he's thinking of moving and ask your advice about where he should move to, making you think you're planning your future together or some shit. He'll "accidentally" leave his weed at your place and you'll see that the name of the weed is "Wedding Cake" so now you associate wedding cake with his dumbass. He'll ask you questions like "Where do you see yourself in ten years?" which you will interpret as him wanting to plan his life with you, and it will take three or four weeks to realize that "Where do you see yourself in ten years?" is a fucking interview question, because these asshole software engineers are too lazy to write a fucking original question into their robot software.

17. Disappears after four months

Once you've severed ties with a robot, or they've severed ties with you after you've made it clear you're going to sever ties with them, the ties get completely severed. You've never seen ties more severed. There isn't a shred left on these ties. After you have your barely 10-minute breakup conversation where, yes, he still asks you "What else is going on?" and says things like, "I think you deserve everything you can get . . ." *Everything I can get? Everything I can get? How about everything I want?* It's another phrase he couldn't get quite right, but you'll be okay with it and you'll even spend the rest of the afternoon rethinking the whole thing.

You'll wonder if you gave up too quickly or maybe you were too cold or maybe he doesn't realize how much fun you did have with him or maybe if you'd said something slightly differently it might still have worked out. And you'll get high and you'll decide you need to be honest with him and let him know that you have conflicting feelings about it all so you'll text him, "Hey, can I talk to you just for five minutes?" And he'll say he can't talk because he's about to leave for the train, and he'll wonder if he can call you tomorrow. Tomorrow. You have literally never asked to talk to him ever about anything. This is the first time. And you just need five minutes. But he doesn't have five minutes now. Maybe tomorrow. And you'll be like, "It's okay, never mind." And he'll go "okay." And that's the LAST YOU'LL EVER HEAR FROM HIM. He will never, for a single second, ever wonder what you were going to say to him. He does not care. He doesn't have the ability to care. Because he's a robot.

If the person you're currently dating displays each and every one these traits, you very well may be dating a robot. Check the back of his neck for a QR code to start your return.

Peace Out,
Monogamy Island

I FELL HEAD OVER HEELS so fast for the first man I dated after my (second) divorce that it scared me. Especially because this guy totally sucked. But he was tall and had a good head of hair and so I started saying things like, "Hmm, maybe I *could* have kids for this guy."

When I was with him I noticed I turned into this person I call "Relationship Sarah."* And I hated Relationship Sarah. Relationship Sarah wasn't me. Relationship Sarah's voice was higher and mousier. Relationship Sarah laughed at things that weren't funny. When I was Relationship Sarah, I wasn't really speaking for myself. I saw everything from his perspective and only said things I thought he wanted to hear. I felt insecure and desperate and also bored but wouldn't dare say any of that out loud. Instead I doubled down, told him I wanted more, wanted to take it further. The second I did, though, he ended it. THANK GOD.† But it scared me how quickly I could fall into a shitty, lonely relationship with someone whose

---

* I just remembered that this is a concept mentioned on *Seinfeld*, in the famous "A George divided against itself cannot stand" speech where George, played by Jason Alexander—who follows me on Twitter, by the way—mentions Independent George and Relationship George. I think I came up with Relationship Sarah independently, but I can't be sure and hope I'm not infringing on any copyrights.

† An alternate title for this memoir was *Rejected by All the Right Men*.

only claim to my heart was hair and height. So I uninstalled all my dating apps. I needed to take a step back and figure out what problem I was really trying to solve.

I decided to try to just meet men in real life and see what happened when I wasn't looking for a relationship.

The first potential player was a barista at the hotel I stayed at while filming *Unfrosted*. It is so clutch to make friends with a barista—free oat milk lattes all the time. He was an actor, too, and we had a few great chats and then he asked for my number. Boom. I was about to have a fling with the barista. The next day I asked what he was up to that weekend, and he said he was going shopping with his girlfriend. He dropped the girlfriend bomb just like on that episode of *Sex and the City*. No fling with this barista. And now I also had to get my lattes from somewhere else.

The next potential player was the business manager of the same hotel, because I am lazy. He was blond and cute and had a great smile and a very legit business card. But he seemed to be able to talk only about hotel management and head count and event planning. I found myself nodding at things I didn't understand and not even wanting to know more about them. So that did not work out. I got free access to a conference room, though.

The third potential connection had the most potential. He was in the industry. And he was cute. And fun. And Irish. He took me to an Irish restaurant and told me about his Irish dog. We had a lovely kiss and I was ready to have a fling with the Irishman, but when I said I wanted to go home with him, he said he wanted to "take things slow."

What?

Take things SLOW?

WHY??????

In that moment, I realized how ridiculous I sounded when I said this over and over again to every guy I dated in my twenties when I had perfect breasts.

I tried to keep in touch with the Irishman without obsessively texting him and getting obsessed with his life. I actively tried to let go of the need to feel chased and worshipped and followed up on and called and begged to be seen again. And I did it. I felt like I wanted to see him again but I never got obsessed with him. So the Irishman did, at least, teach me about having that detachment. But I never saw him again.

A few months later, I was back at home and I ran into a guy I'd gone on one date with but hadn't seen in a year. Half Black, half Jewish, superhot. He came to one of my stand-up shows and we got a drink afterward. He seemed nervous. And awkward. Really smart but trying way too hard to sound smart, which made him seem not that smart. Would not shut up about his job. Had some conspiracy theorist tendencies. Relationship Sarah would have run for the hills—I could never date someone I couldn't see myself marrying. But New Non-relationship Sarah was like, *Who cares? He's hot.* Dude, I totally became a dude.

I ignored everything coming out of his mouth and invited him back to my place. My behavior was blowing my mind. We hung out on my couch, and I was high so everything he said was funny. And I realized that after being married to the whitest white man for so long, I'd forgotten how much I love Black men. I spent most of my life being horny for white supremacy. My internalized racism, my internalized oppression had found its way into my romantic life, and it's hard to know just how much that affected my attraction to white men.

This is why I no longer agree with interracial relationships. I mean, we all should be able to date whoever we want to date, but we should definitely all stop dating white dudes.* There are just too many beautiful Black and Asian women going to really bad

---

* I realize this means white people will have to be in interracial relationships but I'm still working out the details here.

concerts. I once went to a Phish concert for a guy. And I pretended to enjoy myself. It was degrading. Every song was 20 minutes of mansplaining what an instrument sounds like. After the first song, the guy I was with leaned over and said, "Now they're going to play the same song again but this time Trey's gonna be on bass," and I wanted to kill myself. How is that entertainment? Prince could play every single instrument on his songs, but you didn't see him in concert like, "And now, 'Purple Rain' for the seventh time, but this time I'll be on keyboard."

So please, ladies, listen to me. I've dated every white man there is to date. I've had more white guys inside me than a GameStop in the '90s. And I'm here to tell you: It is not worth it. Marriage. Or white guys. And this is how I know: When a white woman dates a Black guy, Black women are protective. They're like, why are you trying to steal our men? But when a Black woman dates a white guy, white women are like, "Oh, Josh? Yeah, you can have him. He only wears flannels and he's brewing beer in his closet. Have fun with that."

I think most men are like Swiss cheese. There are a lot of holes. And they don't know why those holes are there and they're not trying to figure it out, they're just trying to fill them. With music, with sports, with plants. But women, we look at the holes and we put what we want to see there so that they look like a full slice of Havarti. We tell ourselves he's Gouda. He's some other good cheese that's expensive and delicious; I'm sorry, I don't know cheeses. But he's not. He's still Swiss cheese. My point is, most men are at least 80 percent our fantasies of them, not actually them.

I dubbed my new half-Black, half-Jewish boy toy Black Captain America, and we started having amazing sex. I told him what I liked and what I didn't like. I told him my fantasies. I took charge of the sex. And I fell in love with sex all over again. But I also realized I *love* waking up alone. Waking up alone is the best, it's waking up with FREEDOM. You can stretch out, you can get on your phone, you can go back to sleep, you can fart as loud as you want! There is literally nothing better than waking up alone. I told him that. Not about the farting. Just that I wanted to wake up alone. I did what I wanted to do and stopped worrying if he liked it or not.

The only problem with Black Captain America, though, was that *he wanted me to like him.* Just when I thought I was out, monogamy was trying to pull me back in. He was texting me constantly. Leaving voice notes. FaceTiming me. And I was starting to get sucked in. I loved the attention. And I didn't want to be rude. I tried to stay strong. To not respond right away. Train him. And it sort of worked, but as soon as I texted back, he'd FaceTime me. And it started to be such a turnoff. In his behavior, I saw myself at 26. I saw myself at 32. I saw the obsessiveness, the love-bombing. This man was texting me morning, noon, and night. Talking about the future. Professing his love. Even though he barely knew me. And for the first time I could see it wasn't hot, it was toxic. Cue Britney.

So I had to have a little talk with BCA. I told him I was not interested in a monogamous relationship.

"Why not?" he asked.

And at first I wasn't sure exactly what to say, but then it came to me:

"Because I'm fucking a lotta bitches right now."

(I mean, I'm not, but I hope to be. One day.)

PART 3

Humiliation

The Only Teacher
Who Ever Hated Me

I F THERE'S ONE THING A TEACHER'S PET cannot stand it's when a teacher doesn't like them. And my elementary school music teacher did not like me. At all.

His name was Mr. Joynes. Lawrence Joynes. Larry. And, like Larry on *Three's Company* (who some would call the prototypical Larry—me, I would call him that), Mr. Joynes had shaggy black hair and a permanent five o'clock shadow. He wore baggy Dockers and Hawaiian shirts and boat shoes. But most importantly, he held the key to my dreams. For it was he, and he alone, who could confirm for me the one thing I knew I was put on this earth to do. And that was sing. I wanted to be a singer from as young as I can remember memories. I wanted to be Whitney Houston on Halloween and every other day of the year, too. And if you wanted to sing in my day, you had to be in the chorus: an elite group of third through sixth graders bestowed with the greatest honor on earth. Singing. And Mr. Joynes controlled the chorus. And I wanted to be in the chorus. Bad. But there was steep competition. Twenty students auditioning for 16 coveted spots. And I needed Mr. Joynes to give me one of those spots so I could begin my singing career. It was the only way. Okay, there was one other way, the spring musical, but Mr. Joynes controlled that, too. He was a powerful man.

At this point in my life, I believed myself to be a naturally gifted singer. When I went to church and it was time to sing a hymn, I belted every word. For some reason, my mom told me to just mouth the words, but I assumed she meant because she didn't want others to get jealous of my perfect singing voice. So I started lip-synching. That's right, much like Whitney Houston, I learned how to sing (lip-synch) in church. And I was a natural. At lip-synching. Which I thought was singing.

One summer, we went to an amusement park with my cousins and we did one of those music videos where you and your family pretend to play an instrument and form a band and sing a song. I pretended to play guitar and sing lead vocals for "Under the Board-walk." The teenager working the booth remarked how great I was at singing. He meant lip-synching, but I heard "singing." During a talent show I lip-synched "I Wanna Dance with Somebody" while prancing around in black jeans with bright flowers on them that I stole from Charmaine. I felt like the best singer in the world.

The night before my first chorus audition, I told my mom how excited I was.

"Shouldn't you practice?" she asked.

"No, I don't think so." I shrugged.

All I had to do was go into that music room, sing "The Star-Spangled Banner," and let Mr. Joynes hear my beautiful voice. And that's just what I did. The next day, I went into that music room and sang as loud as I could—the louder the better, I figured. Let 'em hear me! The more emotion I let out, the more I scrunch my face, and flail my arms, and fill the room—oh, he's asking me to stop. Okay, that was quick. I said thank you, and away I went, thinking that went really well! I guess I didn't need to finish the song; Mr. Joynes could see my talent from a mile away.

A few days later, Mr. Joynes came into our homeroom class with a nervous flourish and a yellow pad featuring the names of the 16 new chorus members. As he remarked that he was thankful to all who auditioned and it was really a shame he couldn't accept everyone, I squinted at the list to see if I could see my name, but the names were all in cursive and I couldn't read them. But I was pretty sure I saw an S and a C—I was pretty sure I saw my name. When Mr. Joynes was done with his stupid preamble about how not making chorus didn't mean there was anything wrong with you blah blah blah, it was time. Mr. Joynes proceeded to name each new chorus member, one by one. And instead of looking at him as he read the names, I bowed my head, laser focused on a deep scratch in the middle of my wooden desk. I didn't want anyone to know how badly I wanted it. I didn't want anyone to see the wave of shame I felt as I heard name after name called out that wasn't mine. Silently, I reassured myself, *He's gonna say my name next, he's gonna say my name next, my name's gonna be next, my name's definitely gonna be next.* But Mr. Joynes never said my name. Girls left and right squealed in delight as their names were called until—that was it. All the new chorus members had been announced. And I sat in veiled disbelief that I, Sarah Cooper, gifted singer (lip-syncher), had not made the chorus.

And that exact same scene played out every year for *four years in a row*. From third grade to sixth grade, I auditioned for the chorus and never. Once. Made it. Every year I thought it would be my year, and it. Never. Ever. Was. And I knew it had nothing to do with my voice. Because being a bad singer was obviously not something I was. I had a VHS tape of me singing "Under the Boardwalk" perfectly to prove it. I loved singing. How could I be bad at something I love? That didn't make any sense. No, the reason I never made chorus was clear: Mr. Joynes just didn't like me.

How could Mr. Joynes not like me? Teachers LOVED me. Teachers could not *not* like me. I would always raise my hand. I knew they must love that! They could always count on me. I might not know the answer, but I would not stand idly by and watch the teacher ask a question and have no one respond. No way, not on my watch! I knew the success of every class was laid squarely on my shoulders, and I accepted my responsibility with a grave sense of duty. I helped the teacher hand out milk cartons, I drew pictures of my teachers to be featured in the drawing newsletter, I cleaned the chalkboard and the erasers—which I must admit I loved doing; the smell of chalk still gets me going. I was a board-certified teacher's pet. All teachers loved me. Except Mr. Joynes. For some reason I was unable to cast a spell on Mr. Joynes. He was wholly, continually, painfully unimpressed by me. Which obviously made me obsessed with him.

Mr. Joynes introduced me to the Beatles, I had never heard of them before. It was probably impossible for anyone growing up in the 1960s to escape the Beatles, but my immigrant parents certainly didn't introduce me to them; we only listened to reggae and Perry Como. Mr. Joynes was obsessed with the Beatles. He explained to us why people were convinced that Paul McCartney was actually dead. To a seven-year-old kid who didn't know who the hell Paul McCartney was, this was fascinating. He showed us the album cover where Paul isn't wearing shoes and explained to us that it was a British tradition to remove the shoes of the dead. He played some album backward for us. We were supposed to hear some words about death and I think we all pretended to.

Once, Mr. Joynes played "Penny Lane" for the class and we were supposed to draw what we heard in the music. I sat there with my crayons and construction paper ready to impress Mr. Joynes. And when I listened to the song, I saw a bull pulling a cart.[*] So I drew a bull pulling a cart. After the song was over, we each went up to the front of the class to share our drawing and then Mr. Joynes would put the drawing on the board. But when I shared my drawing, he said, rather disdainfully, " 'Penny Lane' made you think of a bull?" And I said yeah. He wasn't pleased. He decided not to put my draw-

---

[*] I don't know if the song actually made me see a bull pulling a cart or a bull pulling a cart was just on my mind because I was addicted to The Oregon Trail.

ing up on the board, instead placing it on my head and balancing it there. I smiled, turning slowly to make sure the drawing didn't fall off my head as I walked back to my chair. I was smiling because I didn't want the other kids to think Mr. Joynes didn't like me. But I also convinced myself that this was just a funny little misunderstanding, one we'd laugh about during chorus, which I was sure to make next time. But when I kept not making chorus, it made me wonder . . . had he never forgiven me for thinking of a bull while listening to "Penny Lane"?

"Penny Lane," I learned later, is a song whose lyrics have lots of imagery, and Mr. Joynes was probably asking us to just draw exactly what we heard. Which explains why a lot of the drawings were firemen and poppies and blue suburban skies. But I didn't realize there was a right and a wrong answer. Sorry, *Mr. Joynes*, sorry for ruining your perfect plan to create a collage of images from your favorite song. Ironically, the song is also about the difficulty in assessing whether our childhood memories are real or fantasy, which makes these memories even more poignant, don't you think?

Then again, maybe that wasn't the reason he didn't like me. Maybe it was in fourth grade when I missed my cue to enter stage left in the evening production of *You're a Good Man, Charlie Brown*. That's right, you heard me, I was in the evening production. There was a daytime production and an evening production, and I was pretty sure the most talented cast was put in the evening, or so I told myself. Anyway, I was very excited about my character: Pigpen. It was a non-singing role. I mean, it *was* a singing role but they told me not to sing. But I *did* get to wear some fun jean overalls and they put baby powder all over me so that when I entered the stage, I could pat myself down and create a perfect Pigpen cloud of dust. But my cue to walk onstage was when Larisa started singing. Yes, Larisa, the goddamn popular blond girl who always made chorus. I was so jealous of her. She was so popular and so pretty and everyone loved her.

She also dated the guy I had a crush on. Sam. Sam and I should have had a whirlwind romance, especially since he was Pigpen for the daytime production.

Anyway, before she started singing, I was supposed to walk on and sit down center stage, and I had a few lines, I think. But I wasn't there. I was in the wing. I lost concentration because I saw Mr. Joynes panicking behind the stage. I had no idea this play was so important to him. He was, like, freaking out, and I was mesmerized. He was looking up at the ceiling, blinking fast, and he looked like he was nervously praying? And then I realized I wasn't supposed to see that, and also I'd missed my cue and they skipped over my lines and she was already singing. I locked eyes with Mr. Joynes and he shooed me angrily onto the stage. Now I was freaking out. I had to improvise. So I walked out in the middle of her song, trying desperately hard not to let anyone notice, staring up at the ceiling pretending that everything was normal. But I didn't get to create the dust cloud of baby powder because that would've probably been distracting. So a known carcinogen just lay there on my body through the entire show. My first stage experience turned out to be an unmitigated disaster. Maybe that's why Mr. Joynes hated me. I single-handedly ruined the evening production of *You're a Good Man, Charlie Brown*.

Or maybe it was what happened in fifth grade ... commonly referred to as "The Butt Slapping Incident of 1987," "Butt Gate," or "The Slap Heard Round the Playground."

I don't know what was going through my brain. That's not true. I do know. I secretly watched one of my friend's dad's porn VHS tapes and someone got their butt slapped and the guy said he liked it and in my feeble fifth-grade mind, I thought, *Is this what Mr. Joynes wants? Is this what will make Mr. Joynes like me? Maybe he just wants his butt slapped?*

The next day on the playground, I came face-to-face, well, face-to-butt, with a golden opportunity.

I was running around the jungle gym with a few friends, and we suddenly found ourselves in front of where Mr. Joynes was standing at the edge of the grass, talking to a few other teachers. I turned away from my friends, and there it was, Mr. Joynes's butt. It was a very flat butt. His khakis were really washed out, almost white. It did not quite match the butt I saw in the porn video, but here it was, nonetheless. And I knew it was a sign, a sign that I should slap his butt. I took a deep breath. I put my right arm high above my head, and then I cracked my palm across Mr. Joynes's flat, khakied butt as hard as I could.

I made significant palm-to-butt contact. And it was done; I had slapped my music teacher on the ass in public and now I knew he'd like me. After I did it, though, I don't know what I was expecting. Maybe I thought he'd laugh. He'd see me as fun. I don't know. He'd talk to me. I'd tell him how badly I wanted to sing. He would realize the talent he'd missed and put me on the chorus immediately. But that's not what happened. What happened was Mr. Joynes whipped around in a fury, bent down to my face, put a finger up to my nose, and in the harshest of harsh tones, said, "If you do that one more time, young lady, you're going straight to the principal's office." Hot, right? I was shaking. I nodded. He turned his back to me. I was mortified. My friends saw it. The other teachers saw it. I'd just done an awful, horrible thing. I had an identity crisis. Sarah Cooper doesn't get in trouble. And yet there I was, practically in trouble. Dangerously adjacent to trouble. Closer to trouble than I'd ever been.

Mr. Joynes and I avoided eye contact after that.

By the time sixth grade rolled around and Mr. Joynes was reading out the names of the new chorus members, I didn't expect my name to be called. I decided to face the fact that I'd never be able to sing and changed my reason for being on earth to "actress." I'm not an actress, I'm a failed singer.

The shame I felt around singing became a huge chip on my shoulder. Something I decidedly could not do despite priding myself on being good at everything. In Drama, I'd always have a part in the fall show, often a lead part. But when it came to the spring musicals, I was nowhere. I was always in "the chorus," which in high school wasn't where I wanted to be. I wanted an actual singing part with solos and shit. But I never got those. *Pippin. Leader of the Pack. Bye Bye Birdie.* Chorus. Chorus. Chorus. One of the girls who always got a lead singing role wrote me a note at the end of one of the spring productions. In it, she said what a great actress I was but how thankful she was that I couldn't sing, or else she wouldn't get to be onstage at all. That ho.

In my twenties I discovered karaoke and took it way too seriously and still do to this day.

When I was 32, I took six weeks of singing lessons. At the end of the six weeks we had a recital. And I made my parents come watch me sing in a recital. Again, I was 32. The song I chose was "I Can't Make You Love Me," by the great Bonnie Raitt. I secretly dedicated it to Mr. Joynes.

Which made it a little awkward when I decided to look old Mr. Joynes up, see what he was doing, begin the painful process of forgiving him for ruining my singing career, and found out he was alive and kicking and serving 40 years on child pornography charges.

And just in case you think I'm making this up in some sick scheme to get back at the man who ruined my singing career, how dare you, what kind of vindictive bitch do you think I am (but yes, I would do that) (I'm kidding, no I wouldn't), here's a snippet from *The Washington Post*, August 28, 2015:

> *A former Montgomery County music teacher was sentenced to 40 years in prison on Friday for sexually abusing 14 young children at an elementary school. At the hearing, Lawrence W. Joynes spoke publicly about his actions for the first time and described himself as ashamed, frightened, and remorse-*

ful. "*I'm so sorry I betrayed your faith and your trust in me,*" *said Joynes, a 27-year veteran of the public school system, addressing his former students in a statement. "I never, ever meant to harm any of you physically or emotionally. For any damage, any shame, any trauma that I've caused, I apologize from the depths of my soul.*"

When I read this, so many thoughts ran through my mind. I felt awful for those children. I feel bad about the girls who always made chorus who I was so jealous of and I wondered if they were hurt by him. Part of me felt relieved that I was not one of his victims. But mostly I kept thinking . . . *Wow. Mr. Joynes was a pedophile and he still* didn't like me?

Maybe I really can't sing.

Thy Mistress Hath Played the Trumpet in My Bed

B Y THE TIME I GOT TO HIGH SCHOOL, I had given up my dreams of being Whitney Houston and moved on to my dreams of being Whitney Houston in *The Bodyguard*.

I trod the boards of the Magruder High School Drama Club, where our director, Mr. Michael D'Anna, made our drama club feel like a home. Mr. D'Anna loved Shakespeare. He saw Kenneth Branagh's *Much Ado About Nothing* and we did that play the next fall. I fell in love with Emma Thompson and Kate Winslet and got obsessed with the Bard, long before it was the name of Google's AI chatbot. If the director loves Shakespeare, you like Shakespeare, too. Even if that love of Shakespeare is based on a movie released by Metro-Goldwyn-Mayer. It also didn't hurt that I got cast in every play.

One of the first, most exciting parts I ever played was Juliet. Romeo was played by this hot junior named Jesse. Jesse and I took rehearsals very seriously. And by rehearsals I mean making out in the hallway. I mean, how could I not love Shakespeare?

After that there was Ophelia, of course. Helena, sure. Lady Macbeth, why not. But my most significant role was as the lead role of Imogen in Shakespeare's little-known tragedy *Cymbeline*. In one scene, I had to read a letter, written by my betrothed, which basically said I was a slut and he wanted nothing to do with me. The line was "Thy mistress, Pisanio, hath played the strumpet in my bed." A strumpet is a whore. It is also a British pastry. Oops, no, that's a crumpet. Anyway, I was supposed to read this line with shock and sadness and grief, with tears in my eyes, but when I read it, I kept saying, "Thy mistress, Pisanio, hath played . . . the trumpet in my bed." Because it always got a laugh and it was the only laugh we ever got in the whole play. Again, *Cymbeline* is a tragedy.

Mr. D'Anna was frustrated with me. He instructed me do an exercise. An acting exercise. To get at the heart of the scene. To truly become Imogen and wrestle with her shame. Acting exercises are VERY SERIOUS. I sat in a chair in the center of the stage. The other actors walked around me in a circle, calling me a slut, a whore, all kinds of awful names. Hot, right? This was more hilarious than the trumpet thing. I didn't feel ashamed. I couldn't stop laughing.

LAUGHTER WAS CURRENCY in the Cooper household. If you could make someone laugh you could do whatever you wanted. Mom could always make Dad laugh and vice versa. I could usually make Rachael laugh. Charmaine could always make me laugh. George was just always laughing. Even as a child, I found that I could ease any tension at home with a well-timed quip.

Growing up, my sisters and I watched *Reading Rainbow* and *Sesame Street*. I loved Kermit. At night we watched *Showtime at the Apollo* and loved Sinbad. We watched Benny Hill reruns. We were also obsessed with *In Living Color*. One of our favorite sketches was "Hey Mon," about a hardworking West Indian family. I was going to describe one of the sketches here, but you should just go watch it. Those sketches cracked us up and felt accurate as hell. Papa Hedley *was* my dad. Charmaine would say, "You lazy lima bean!" and I'd say, "But mi have tree job!" My sisters and I were also big on sitcoms. My first celebrity crush was Jack Tripper on *Three's Company*. I could watch John Ritter try to get into or out of a hammock forever. I still swoon when I hear, "Come and knock on our door." We loved *The*

Cosby Show. We would tape it* and watch the episodes over and over again—especially the one where the family lip-synched "(Night Time Is) the Right Time" by Ray Charles. I credit that as one of my early lip-synching influences, along with Gospel hymns and "Under the Boardwalk." In high school and beyond, my comedic sensibilities were honed on a strict diet of *This Is Spinal Tap, Best in Show,* and the entire Naked Gun cinematic universe. The scene where she tries to slap Leslie Nielsen with one hand, and then the other, and then a third hand comes up from the bottom out of nowhere and slaps him—so good. It's not just the gag, it's Leslie Nielsen's look of utter shock, in a way that's still goofy enough that you know no one is going to explain where that hand came from. We never see it again and we just laugh and don't care. God, who cares about things that make sense. Things that don't make sense are more fun.

MR. D'ANNA HELPED ME get a theater scholarship to the University of Maryland. But when I got to college and started doing theater it wasn't as easy as I thought it was going to be. I hated the dance requirement. And my parents were pushing me to do something more practical. They thought I should do business. I wanted to play a part onstage, and they wanted me to literally become a different person. A person who understands money. They wanted me to go Method, like Marlon Brando, Daniel Day-Lewis type shit. Mr. D'Anna didn't teach us that. I was like, Mom, Dad, the acting skills I'd need to get a degree in business would require a degree in theater.

I compromised. I changed my major to economics, which is like business theater. I auditioned for a part in a main stage production, but when I got the part, I backed out so I could focus on my senior thesis titled "The Economic Viability of Private Prisons." I really committed to the bit.

---

* Using a technology called "VHS."

My TED Talk Vibe

SOMETIME IN 2018, I was taking a stroll around Brooklyn when I saw an artist selling his work on the sidewalk. He had a very unique marketing technique. A woman walked by, and he yelled out, "Hey, mami, come take a look!" Another woman walked by, and he yelled out, "Hey, sis, check this out!" A man walked by, and he yelled out, "Hey, cousin, I have something for you!" He was really appealing to their familial natures. *And aren't we all family,* I thought, deeply and introspectively, because I am deep and introspective. I am also a giant loser, because in just a few seconds, *I* would be walking by him, and I started to get a little excited wondering which family member I'd be. Was I a mami? Was I a sis? I could be a sis! Or a cousin? Or . . . god no, I hope not an auntie, I hate being called "auntie." It feels derogatory. I don't like being called the A-word.

But when I walked by, he didn't call me the A-word. He called me something so much worse.

He looked at me and said, "Hey, teacher!"

TEACHER?

I'm not even good enough to be a family member? And worse, I'm a teacher? I looked him dead in the face and yelled, "Fuck you, dude!"

Just kidding, of course I did not do that. It would set a bad example. What kind of lesson would that be? I just kept walking. But I couldn't stop thinking about it. Why was I a teacher? What about me said teacher? I was in my normal Ann Taylor Loft attire. I had sensible shoes on. My hair was in a bun. WHAT THE FUCK ABOUT ME SAID TEACHER?

I know some of you out there, especially my sister-in-law, Susie, would say, What's wrong with being mistaken for a teacher, it's an honor! And I agree, it is an honor. I love teachers. You *know* this. But you don't understand, being mistaken for a teacher is something I've been trying to outrun my entire life. I call it my TED Talk vibe. When I talk, people think they need to start taking notes; they're always expecting slides and takeaways.

It's true, I have all the hallmark traits of a teacher. Studious. Follows all the rules. Type A control freak. Smart. Warm but condescending, hard to read, diplomatic, empathetic, a very convincing fake smile.

But I could change all that if I wanted to. I mean, I wasn't going to, but I *could*. And yet, here was this man, who didn't know anything about me at all, and he instinctively sensed my teacher vibe. This meant that my teacheryness went deep. And it triggered me. Because 10 years prior, I took an acting class where the teacher looked me dead in the face and in front of everyone told me I'd only ever be cast as a teacher. Or a student. Or a student teacher. That's right, she banished me to acting in *exclusively academic environments*. And it haunts me to this day.

IT WAS 2008. I was living in San Francisco. I had just left my job at Yahoo! to pursue my acting dream. And I knew exactly where to start: Yelp. Which is where I found Shelley Mitchell's acting class. I was single, childless, jobless, and ready to be catapulted to stardom before I turned the ripe old age of 30. I called up Shelley and said, "Hey, Shelley, I want to come to your class." She told me her class was a bit different, it wasn't for everyone, which made me think she thought I couldn't handle it, so I was definitely in. I've never met a class I couldn't conquer.

I said, "Challenge accepted, Shelley" (silently to myself) and told her I'd be there.

Shelley's class was in a small, dark room of an apartment in a walk-up in the Mission. This is where I came face-to-face with her for the first time. One of the most intimidating human beings on earth. The kind of person who can see right through your bullshit from a mile away. The kind of teacher I was desperate to impress with my bullshit.

There was a small stage at the front of the room. We often started class with an Important Acting Exercise called "chair work." In this exercise, the actor sits in a chair on the stage. And cries. Okay, the point was not to cry, I didn't know what the point was. So I sat there trying to cry.

I did a monologue from *When Harry Met Sally*. After I was done she asked me if the movie was a comedy. I said yes. She asked me if I noticed anyone laughing. I said no.

Once she assigned me a monologue of a character who smoked. I dove headfirst into my new identity as a smoker. I went to the store and bought a pack of Virginia Slims. I was so excited to impress Shelley with my fantastic prop work. I got onstage. I balanced a Slim elegantly between my fingers. I pretended to take a drag. I opened my mouth to begin the monologue. Shelley stopped me before I even said a word.

"Have you ever smoked a cigarette before?" she asked.

"Oh god no, never," I said with pride.

"Oh, so you look down on smokers?" she said. "You look down on the character you're trying to portray?"

I was confused. Wasn't I holding the cigarette the right way? I'm pretty sure I was, I looked it up on YouTube.

The following week, I improvised a monologue about what it was like to work in tech, how I just felt stuck inside a box. She told me I should turn it into a one-woman show. But I didn't want to do that, I wanted to be a star.

I did a silent monologue as my mother. I got onstage and looked at myself in an imaginary mirror the way I often saw my mom doing. I sucked in my stomach the way she would, I turned to the side the way I'd seen her do many times. Shelley told me it was the most truthful thing I'd done in class and I should keep going with it. But I didn't want to play my mother, I wanted to be a star. It took my stubborn ass years to embrace myself as a stand-up comedian who had lots of observations about tech and impressions of my mom.

In that class I discovered Stella Adler, August Wilson, *The Drama of the Gifted Child*, *The Book: On the Taboo Against Knowing Who You Are*, and I carried those books everywhere and read many parts of them. I discovered the magic of repetition. I learned meditation and how to quiet the voice in my head by saying to myself, "I wonder what my next thought will be?" Which was all well and good, but I still wanted to be a star.

I told Shelley I was going to move to Los Angeles and start auditioning. And that's when she said I'd probably only ever play a teacher or a student.

And I had to prove her wrong. I had to prove to her that I wasn't a straitlaced Goody Two-shoes, I was a star! I was wild, I was unpredictable, I was uncontrollable! And the only way to do this, of course, was to elope with one of the other students in her class and throw away my whole life for a douche canoe. Yeah, that would show her.

Now as you read the next paragraph, I want you to circle all the red flags. There will be a pop quiz at the end.

This guy walks into my acting class, and he's dressed in a three-piece double-breasted white suit and he's wearing sunglasses even though it's nine p.m. And within a week of knowing me he tells me he's in love with me. He proposes to me in a Chinese restaurant, in a strip mall, off the highway, after his podiatry appointment. For his birthday I took him to see his favorite . . . band? No, pastor, Joel Osteen. We went to Joel Osteen's church, and I pretended to be raptured. Joel Osteen came over and I shook and fainted, and they were so impressed, and I was like, wow, if only Shelley could see me now! My revenge fiancé didn't really understand sarcasm. Or irony. He had a 24 Hour Fitness membership and took those hours seriously. He taught me how to make his martini but it was never good enough. And he slept in only a cut-off T-shirt. Let me repeat: *only* a cut-off T-shirt. It was like a Winnie-the-Pooh cosplay. And he was uncircumcised, so every morning I'd wake up to a big dick in a little T-shirt and a little dick in a little T-shirt.

How many red flags did you count? That's right, there were 18 million.

In Shelley's class, my new fiancé and I did a scene together from *The Piano*. And as thankful as I am that this began my lifelong love affair with Jane Campion, I am even more thankful that there is no way Jane Campion can ever see that performance.

After three months of wedded non-bliss, I wound up asking for a divorce and moving back in with my parents. It wasn't LA, it was Atlanta (my parents had followed me to Atlanta when I was working at IQTV and they were still there) but I started doing extra work and auditioning for TV and film, and wouldn't you know it? The first role I got was in an independent movie as . . . a teacher.

I feel like Shelley cursed me.

She's the reason that when I go to the grocery store, the clerk asks me for my teacher discount card. I don't have one. And the reason that when I go to the museum, kids gather around me in a circle, but I don't know them. And the reason that when I walk by street artists who don't know me at all, they yell out, "Teacher!"

But I wasn't going to take it. I wanted a second opinion. From the same guy. I wanted one more opinion from the same guy who gave me the bad opinion. So I turned around. And walked back and passed him again and waited for the nickname. But instead I heard . . . "Hello, Sarah."

He stood. And he slowly pulled off his mask, *Scooby-Doo* style.

And it was no male street artist at all. It was Shelley Mitchell. She'd been following me around for 10 years. Pretending to be different people in my life. The grocer, the kids at the museum, this artist on the street. Just to reinforce this stereotype she placed on me. Just so I would believe she was right. And leave a good review on her Yelp page. She had a reputation to protect. And I fell for it.

And she just laughed and laughed and laughed.

Okay, that last part might've been a sativa-induced fever dream.

When I got to Shelley's class, I didn't even know what I was doing. I just thought that if I could do it perfectly, Shelley would like me and tell me I was going to be a star. She did not do that. Because being perfect and acting don't go together at all. Turns out, in acting class, trying to impress the teacher makes for some pretty shitty performances.

There was one moment where Shelley asked me to think of a justification for a line. And I did, and I wrote it down, and I was just about to tell her what I wrote down when I stopped myself. I realized I only wanted to tell her to impress her, and it wasn't necessary. I realized she didn't need to know what I wrote down. It was just for me. If it works, it works, and if it doesn't, it doesn't, but either way, it's just for me. And not to impress her. Which I'm pretty sure really impressed her.

Shelley taught me what learning really is. It's like, you know, learning. And not trying to impress anyone. Thank you for coming to my TED Talk vibe.

Journal: Noogler to Googler to Xoogler

T HE FOLLOWING IS AN EXCERPT from the journal I kept when I was 36. I was living with Jeff in the East Village and planning our wedding and I had just left Google.

October 20, 2014

My last day at Google was Friday. I feel like such a fucking idiot for leaving. I had most people telling me I shouldn't leave. My fiancé, my family, my therapist. At the final hour, I signed up for a life coaching class. I had one session, and told my story of how I was about to leave Google to pursue writing. The coach's only advice to me, and the only sort of non-supportive advice she gave the entire session was—don't quit your job yet. I had a one on one with my boss right after that. I almost said something about not wanting to quit. But then I didn't. I went to San Juan to look at the wedding venue and woke up in the middle of the night about to email a former manager of mine to see if I could join her team. But I calmed myself down. And I ended up going through with it. I wrote thank you cards to everyone on my team. It's so weird how you have no idea how much people mean to you until you are saying goodbye to them. It's such a fucked up part of human nature. I had started to sort of resent this place because I didn't feel creative, and I couldn't do what I wanted to do—which was write. And yet, I didn't think about all the writing I had still been doing even with a fulltime job. They say if you want something done, you should give it to someone busy. And now I'm not busy anymore. I'm just sitting here. Writing. Not missing the work so much as just missing having the place to go, the assignment to complete. The free food to partake of. I realize now how much of my identity was wrapped up in Google. How I had this secret notion that I was better than everyone because I worked at Google. I felt important. I felt smart. And I really took that for granted. Not that it's a good thing. I don't want to be so wrapped up in where I work that I don't have an identity of my own. But I guess it's too fresh now, and I still don't really know who I am or what I want to do, so there's just an emptiness. My old guitar teacher mentioned something like this. About how when you let things go that you've held on to for so long, it feels very uncomfortable. He was talking about my focus on finding a man at the time. And all my online dating excursions. He told me I should stop doing that, and focus on myself. And that it would feel uncomfortable. That there were conversations I couldn't fall back on, which I noticed right away. I didn't feel like talking about guys with my girlfriend anymore, and yet it seemed like our entire relationship was built on that, and now—what were we going to talk about. It's like that when you quit a job and you don't really have a job. And I went from having THE job to having no job. And I've done this before. And yet before I wasn't worried at all. Maybe it's just because I've gotten older. Maybe things feel more important and maybe because I'm getting married now I feel like I might not just be fucking up my life alone anymore. And I'm not fucking up my life, I don't think, it just feels that way. And I get this way, I judge myself. When I was at Google, if I had a bad stand-up show it didn't matter *because, whatever, I work at Google. Now if I write an article and it doesn't do well, or if I put up a video, or if I do a show, and it doesn't go well, guess what, I shouldn't have quit my day job, but I already did! I have nothing else. Just me. That's all I've got. And that's scary. And it's very uncomfortable. There's this desire to give up before I even try. It's not so much that I feel pressure to make money, I just feel pressure to not look like an idiot. And not look stupid for doing something that most people would never do. It's weird how everyone tells you you're doing the right thing. They're all like yeah, you want to jump so you should jump, I wish I could jump, but no I can't ever jump. But you should definitely jump. You're really inspiring all of us to jump too but we would never actually do that.*

I don't know. I guess it's some weird twist of fate and psychology that I'm sitting here now, jobless, Google-title-less, with all the time I need, with enough money, with a vocation I can do anywhere for anyone, and I'd like to just shoot myself in the foot and think about how I shouldn't be here and I'm an idiot and try to figure out how to get back to Google as soon as possible. Maybe all those people who told me I shouldn't quit knew who I am more than I know who I am. They know that I'll never be a real artist, I'll always be a wannabe who actually needs and succeeds best when the man is telling me what to do and I'm delivering it.

But there is something so scary and sad too about always doing what other people want you to do. Do this job, get this money, go home and try to find some time for yourself if you can. Come back in the morning. Don't get me wrong, if you are going to do that anywhere, Google is the place to do it. But I get worried about living my whole life that way. Maybe I just need to find peace in it somehow. I know when I'm the happiest is when I'm making things and seeing how people react to them, especially if that reaction involves laughing. Or even just identifying with it.

Or even if they don't get the joke and they take it seriously, that's pretty rewarding too. And in the goodbye video that my team put together for me, it's obvious I won't be remembered for my design leadership, I'm laughing now just thinking about it. It was bad how little I cared by the end. I just didn't care anymore. And when you're surrounded by people who care sooo much, it's just hard to try and fake it and if you're not faking it you're probably pissing people off, I don't know. I always just faked it. And I couldn't fake it anymore. I didn't want to. And I didn't want to not be able to say whatever I want to say in my writing either. God I think this whole time I just wanted to really be myself and have everyone see that. And everyone saw that at work. And they're so supportive of me. And they believe in me more than I believe in myself. Which is weird.

Six more minutes. I can write for six more minutes. Today I need to get a few things done but otherwise take it easy. There are things I'm excited about. I would love to get on TV again. I really enjoy that. I would love to write an article that goes viral again. I would love to start my Cooper Review show. That would be fun. Maybe if I think about my week in terms of all the opportunities there are, instead of what I'm not getting (free food, a paycheck, the chance to see my fiancé all day) then I'll be able to actually be happy. And enjoy this time, for however long it lasts this time. Which might be 6 months, or it could be 6 years. Or maybe the rest of my life. The more I cherish it the longer it will last. I want to cherish it while I have it, not only when I have to say goodbye to it. I wonder if I could turn this into an article somehow. I don't know. I'd probably need to edit it heavily. I need an editor.

Is This Funny?

THE FIRST TIME I DID STAND-UP was at an open mic at the Laughing Skull Lounge in Atlanta. I was 32 and had just moved back in with my parents after eloping with, then divorcing, that guy. I had a lot of material.

At that point, I'd only seen stand-up live once. And that was Mitch Hedberg many years earlier when I was dragged to a show by my boss Adam and spent the rest of that summer saying things like, "Have you ever tried playing tennis with a wall? They are relentless."

To be honest, the only reason I tried stand-up was because acting wasn't working out. I was auditioning but booking nothing. I knew I needed to find my captial-T Truth. I thought stand-up would make me a better Actor. But then I got hooked on just trying to be myself.

When the host called my name that night, I was shaking. Thankfully I was also really drunk. I opened with a one-liner: "I love being single because it makes it easier for me to cry myself to sleep." And it got a laugh! And that felt incredible. Then I told a story about a guy I was dating. The big punch line was, "I'm fucking a lotta bitches right now." It got several laughs. I showed my mom the video of that first time and she told me I shouldn't be speaking like that in public. But I didn't listen. I started doing open mics. I watched fellow Atlanta comedians Dulcé Sloan, Shalewa Sharpe, and Baron Vaughn in awe. I moved to New York, where I sold tickets to comedy shows for stage time. I loved watching Marina Franklin, Gary Gulman, and Phil Hanley, and YouTube clips of Donald

Glover and Chelsea Peretti. For me, being onstage was often an out-of-body experience, but I lived for those moments when I felt totally present, like I was just being myself.

Since then, stand-up comedy has taken me to a lot of places. To basements, to bringers, to bar shows. To classes with Rick Crom at the Comedy Cellar, to hosting open mics, to producing and hosting my own bar shows. To *Kimmel*. To the DC Improv on my own tour. To the Beacon, 12 years later, opening for Chelsea Handler on her Vaccinated and Horny tour, where I met my idols Amy Schumer and Sarah Silverman for the first time. That was the first time my mom got to see me perform live. She was okay with the language that time.

I always liked writing stand-up more than performing it. I have so many random notes jotted down like "I believe gay people invented marriage to turn straight people gay." But sitting down to work on those bits, then taking my ass to a club to try those bits, was like pulling teeth. I still get nervous before going onstage and I still don't really know why some things work and some things don't. I believe it lies in a perfect marriage of text and tone, which is the holy grail I'm always looking for. And I love that my writing evolves as I do, and that my writing helps me evolve. I never saw myself in tech for the rest of my life but I see that with writing. I love that I could have this same job when I'm 90 and hopefully be talking about some great sex I had with a 70-year-old. Okay, maybe I won't evolve that much.

I could explain to you where I get my material, but now that you've gotten to know me a little bit, I think you'll see where these little bits came from.

———————————————

"Jamaican Parents"

I was born in Jamaica and my whole family is Jamaican.

And I think the hardest thing about being a Jamaican in America is:

I am Black, but then again . . . am I?

I consider myself Black but no one else does.

So I had this terrible identity crisis growing up.

I was always the only Black kid at the Poison concert.

My parents always said, We're not Black, we're Jamaican.

They're kind of like Bruce Willis in *The Sixth Sense*.

He didn't know he was dead, and my parents don't realize that they're Black.

Like, I'd be walking around a mall with my dad and he'd say, "Look, Sarah, look at those Black people over there."

And I'd say, "Dad, that's a mirror."

"The Audition"

I really wanted to be an actress when I was little.

When I was in my twenties and I got my first agent

I started getting sent out on all these roles that just weren't right for me.

My agent called me once and she said,

"Sarah, I have this audition for you but you gotta be Black for this one, you gotta really be Black, you gotta dig deep."

So I showed up late.

And this is what happened:

Hi!!! I'm Sarah Cooper and I'm going to be reading for the role of Shaqueefwa Jones!!!

I just had a few questions about the monologue.

Do I really have to say the N-word here, because people don't even really talk like that—oh they do? They do talk like that? Okay.

And then it says she struts in loosely, is that like ballerina loose?

Oh prostitute loose. Okay. Be a Black hooker. I can do that! So much fun!!!

I just, you know, I just don't want to feed into any negative stereotypes.

Oh you want me to feed into those? Okay I can do that!! Okay here goes.

[Backs up, does a slow, bowlegged strut to the mic, and says in the whitest voice I can muster]

Yo, boy! You best come get these gotdamn kids up out this gotdamn house before I bussa cap in your—

Oh you've heard enough? You've heard enough? Okay, great.

Well thank you so much for the opportunity.

It is such an honor auditioning for *the* Tyler Perry.

You're not Tyler Perry?

———————————————

"Interracial Marriage"

I'm in an interracial marriage.

I'm Black and my husband is a software engineer at Google.

He's white, he's really white, he's *hard-H* whhhhite.

His middle name is de Blanc.

And if you know French you know "de Blanc" means "All Lives Matter."

And that's a family name, his great-great-great-great-great-grandfather was Jean Maxmillian Alcibiadies Derneville de Blanc.

Around town he was just known as Chad.

And Chad was the founder of the Knights of the White Camelia, which was like the KKK of Louisiana.

And so when I got married, I quit my job, because reparations.

And every morning he'd go to work and I'd sleep all day and I'd be like, who's the slave now, bitch?

"Male Cheerleaders"

Did you know that the first cheerleaders were men?

They called themselves cheer leaders, two words.

They called themselves leaders, because they wanted to feel important.

They knew it would look good on LinkedIn.

We all know that if the first cheerleaders were women, they would have been called "cheer assistants."

Legend has it that these male cheer leaders would cheer for women's sports, too.

But the cheers were a bit different. They'd go like this:

Be aggressive! Be-e aggressive!

Not THAT aggressive, you're making me feel uncomfortable.

Why don't you smile some more?

That is what your face is for.

Be submissive! Be-e submissive! Yeah!

"Accidental Orgasms"

I wish I was a man so I knew what it felt like to accidentally have an orgasm.

I want to know what it feels like to have an orgasm,

without trying very hard to have an orgasm.

I've never accidentally had an orgasm.

I've accidentally started crying on a plane.

But all my orgasms are 100% deliberate, through extreme concentration and focus.

Men, the level of concentration it takes me to have an orgasm is like what it takes you to just listen without trying to offer a solution. It's a lot.

I don't need female Viagra, I need Adderall.

"'77 Cooper"

I am going through a divorce.

And I'm trying to figure out how to say that in a sexy way.

Because I'm single now and I need to be sexy if I ever want to have sex again.

But when I try to say it sexy I feel like a used-car salesman:

[used-car salesman voice]

Can I interest you in a '77 Cooper?

Let me tell you about our certified pre-owned pussy.

It's still got that new pussy smell.

It's hardly been used.

The last driver was asleep at the wheel.

We were on a quarterly system toward the end there.

That's right, has not been driven since Q1.

The last time the keys were in this ignition was way before the R. Kelly documentary came out.

She takes regular lube, nothing fancy.

She's got one gray hair in between her headlights, but we are working on that.

And if you'd like to take her for a test drive, I will need to see proof of insurance, driver's license, and employment history.

"Birthday Presents"

I had a birthday recently and my friends came over and they got me some presents.

My presents were: one vibrator and four daily planners.

So I have one friend who thinks I'm cool and fun, and four who know me.

The gifts are perfect, actually, because, yes, I'm excited by orgasms but I'm even more excited by time management.

I haven't used the vibrator yet but I have scheduled time to use it.

My friend was like, When are you gonna use it? When are you gonna use it?

And I was like, Next Tuesday between 2 and 2:05.

It's a vibrator, I figured I should put it in a tight slot.

"The Feast of Saint Sarah"

I've noticed that men are really excited to go down on me, because, obviously.

But I know it's because they simply have no idea what they're up against.

They don't know the enemy.

They get down there, they get lost, they give up before the battle is won.

I realized that what men need is a speech.

You know, like a *Rudy*-style speech.

Like *Braveheart*, you know?

To really prepare them for the battle ahead.

So I came up with this:

[slight British accent]

This battle will be long.

Yea, your tongue must be longer.

The airless dungeon that awaits you now may send your mind into a madness.

You may get down there and start to wonder, Who am I? Where am I? And wish to God you'd gone home with someone else.

But he who doesn't have the stomach for this fight, let him find an Uber now!

For this battle is called the Feast of Saint Sarah.

He who outlives this hour—yes, *hour*—will have a valiant story to share with all his homies!

And he shall hold his head high, and show his sore chin, and say, This wound . . . I had on Saint Sarah's hour!

Now, charge!

THE LIFE OF A COMEDIAN

10 Tricks to Appear Smart
in Meetings

I'VE ALWAYS BEEN AN EXTREMELY COMPETITIVE PERSON over the dumbest things. Is this true for you, too? And if so, who does it better? Answer the five questions below to find out now.

Question One

Do you always look at the "To" line of a group email to see what order everyone is in? Have you ever looked at it and noticed you were last and it pissed you off so much that you went through *each and every person* who was listed before you, evaluating your performance in relation to theirs and wondering how this could have happened, and then became filled with so much spite that you immediately *deleted* the email because obviously if you weren't important enough to be put at least *second or third* then why even bother reading it, but then you undelete it and respond first so that at least your name will be at the top of the email thread?

Answer: YES. NO.

Question Two

Has a coworker ever complained about how many unread emails they had, but in a way it was obvious they were actually *bragging* about it, so you tried to one-up them by saying you had so many unread emails, too, *like a hundred,* but then they say *that's nothing,*

I have like two hundred fifty, and you kick yourself for being the idiot who threw a number out first, because now this person thinks they're more important than you?

Answer: YES. NO.

Question Three
Have you ever given a group presentation and afterward you get a bunch of compliments, but you notice it's always about the parts of the presentation *you didn't do* and you start to keep track of who compliments you on the things *you did do* so you know who's really on your side?

Answer: YES. NO.

Question Four
Have you ever gone to a restaurant with your coworker and the waiter comes over and pours her water first and you're like, *What the fuck, dude? Am I not white enough for your racist ass?* (Even though your coworker is also Black.) So you want to make him feel *extra* guilty for not pouring your water first, so you tip him 30 percent and then you come back every week until he pours your water first?

Answer: YES. NO.

Question Five
Have you ever posted a tweet expressing concern over a global catastrophe and had someone respond that you should "get off Twitter for a while" and then 50 people like that response so you spend the next hour blocking that person and every person who liked it?

Answer: YES. NO.

If you answered yes to any of these, I bet I could still beat you in responding to a baby announcement email with "Congratulations! So precious!"

My extremely-competitive-over-dumb-shit nature led me to write an article, which later became an illustrated article, which later became a book, which later became a calendar, called "10 Tricks to Appear Smart in Meetings."

In corporate America there is no greater competitive battlefield than the meeting.

In meetings, I prided myself on being someone who contributed nothing but still seemed absolutely essential. My technique for this was just to make confused faces every now and then. And nodding, of course, lots of nodding. But one day, someone appeared smarter than me by doing *only slightly more than that.*

It was Santa Clara, California. The Valley of the Silicon; 2007. A brightly lit Yahoo! conference room and a meeting of about 10 discussing something I don't think any of us would give a fuck about now. Something extraordinary happened. I saw a product manager get up to draw something on the whiteboard. What was it? We all watched in silence. And as he stepped back from the whiteboard, what he drew came into focus. It was a Venn diagram that made absolutely no sense.

But instead of everyone laughing at him and telling him he was wasting time, something else extraordinary happened. One by one, people started chiming in about how to make the Venn diagram more accurate, make this circle bigger, make this one smaller, change the labels.

It infuriated me. Everyone was impressed with *this*? I sat in bewildered awe as this product manager handed the marker to someone else, sat back down in his chair, and returned to his laptop as everyone else obsessed over this ridiculous Venn diagram.

I had to remember this trick. So I wrote in my notebook:

How to look smart in a meeting: draw a Venn diagram.

A week or so later, I was in another meeting. And the person presenting was talking about click-through rate, or CTR as they call it (to look smart). They said, "About twenty-five percent of people clicked on this button."

And someone else in the meeting said, "Oh, so about one in four." And everyone nodded. I could tell they were all secretly impressed with this guy's quick math skills. Yet he, in no way, shape, or form, added anything remotely valuable to the meeting. So I wrote it down in my notebook:

Translate percentages into fractions.

And I put that notebook away until seven years later. I was moving in with my boyfriend, and I came across the notebook again. At that point I was working as a design manager for Google and I was in so many meetings and becoming infuriated each day as I watched people do absolutely nothing and still look smart. So I decided to finish that list.

On June 30, 2014, I posted this article on Medium:

10 Tricks to Appear Smart in Meetings

Like everyone, appearing smart in meetings is my top priority. Sometimes this can be difficult if you start daydreaming about your next vacation, your next nap, or bacon. When this happens, it's good to have some fallback tricks to fall back on. Here are my ten favorite tricks for quickly appearing smart in meetings.

1. Draw a Venn diagram

Getting up and drawing a Venn diagram is a great way to appear smart. It doesn't matter if your Venn diagram is wildly inaccurate, in fact, the more inaccurate the better.

Even before you've put that marker down, your colleagues will begin fighting about what exactly the labels should be and how big the circles should be, etc. At this point, you can slink back to your chair and go back to playing Candy Crush on your phone.

2. **Translate percentage metrics into fractions**

If someone says, "About 25% of all users click on this button," quickly chime in with, "So about 1 in 4," and make a note of it. Everyone will nod their head in agreement, secretly impressed and envious of your quick math skills.

3. **Encourage everyone to "take a step back"**

There comes a point in most meetings where everyone is chiming in, except you. Opinions and data and milestones are being thrown around and you don't know your CTA from your OTA. This is a great point to go, "Guys, guys, guys, can we take a step back here?" Everyone will turn their heads toward you, amazed at your ability to silence the fray. Follow it up with a quick, "What problem are we really trying to *solve*?" and, boom! You've bought yourself another hour of looking smart.

4. **Nod continuously while pretending to take notes**

Always bring a notepad with you. Your rejection of technology will be revered. Take notes by simply writing down one word from every sentence that you hear. Nod continuously while doing so. If someone asks you if you're taking notes, quickly say that these are your own personal notes and that someone else should really be keeping a record of the meeting. Bravo, compadre. You've saved your ass, and you've gotten out of doing any extra work. Or any work at all, if you're truly succeeding.

5. **Repeat the last thing the engineer said, but very, very slowly**

Make a mental note of the engineer in the room. Remember their name. They'll be quiet throughout most of the meeting, but when their moment comes everything out of their mouth will spring from a place of unknowable brilliance. After they utter those divine words, chime in with, "Let me just repeat that," and repeat exactly what the engineer just said, but very, very slowly. Now that engineer's brilliance has been transferred to you. People will look back on the meeting and mistakenly attribute the intelligent statement to you.

6. **Ask "Will this scale?" no matter what it is**

It's important to find out if things will scale no matter what it is you're discussing. No one even really knows what that means, but it's a good catchall question that generally applies and drives engineers nuts.

7. **Pace around the room**

Whenever someone gets up from the table and walks around, don't you immediately respect them? I know I do. It takes a lot of guts but once you do it, you immediately appear smart. Fold your arms. Walk around. Go to the corner and lean against the wall. Take a deep, contemplative sigh. Trust me, everyone will be shitting their pants wondering what you're thinking. If only they knew (bacon).

8. **Ask the presenter to go back a slide**

"Sorry, could you go back a slide?" They're the seven words no presenter wants to hear. It doesn't matter where in the presentation you shout this out, it'll imme-

diately make you look like you're paying closer attention than everyone else is, because clearly *they* missed
the thing that you're about to brilliantly point out. Don't
have anything to point out? Just say something like,
"I'm not sure what these numbers mean," and sit back.
You've bought yourself almost an entire meeting of appearing smart.

9. **Step out for a phone call**

You're probably afraid to step out of the room because
you fear people will think you aren't making the meeting a priority. Interestingly, however, if you step out of a
meeting for an "important" phone call, they'll all realize just how busy and important you are. They'll say,
"Wow, this meeting is important, so if he has something
even *more* important than this, well, we better not
bother him."

10. **Make fun of yourself**

If someone asks what you think, and you honestly didn't
hear a single word anyone said for the last hour, just say,
"I honestly didn't hear a single word anyone said for the
last hour." People love self-deprecating humor. Say things
like, "Maybe we can just use the lawyers from my divorce," or "God, I wish I was dead." They'll laugh, value
your honesty, consider contacting HR, but most importantly, they'll think you're the smartest-looking person in
the room.

At work, everyone was talking about the article, and they were
very much all flattered to be even tangentially written about. A few
people started pitching me their own tricks to appear smart in

meetings, like Ryan, who would schedule a meeting and show up late to his own meeting, thereby making everyone wait for him and realize how important he was. I had found something that really resonated with people. Inspired, I started my own blog called *The Cooper Review* and began posting office humor and anything else I could come up with. I sent out email newsletters. I made videos. I sold merch. And it all started from "10 Tricks to Appear Smart in Meetings." This one article caused people to literally give up their tricks for the taking! I thought for sure this meant the end of all bullshit in meetings and reinstatement of the proper order of me looking the smartest without really doing anything. I was wrong.

After the article came out, I was in a meeting at Google with about 12 people. Our director was pacing around the room, *and then* he asked the presenter to go back a slide—he was doing two of my tricks at the *same time*. He looked over at me and winked. He read the article! He was brazenly doing my tricks right in front of me and no one said a word. Two weeks later, he was promoted to VP. Coincidence? I don't think so.

On October 16, 2016, I published my first book: *100 Tricks to Appear Smart in Meetings*. Two weeks later, Donald Trump was elected president. Coincidence? Yeah, probably.

How to President

HOW DID A JAMAICAN GIRL grow up to be the president of the United States? Well, it's a spellbinding tale that involves zero intrigue and absolutely no international espionage, unless you think TikTok is international espionage, which: valid.

My 2020 started out a little rocky but otherwise hunky-dory. I was living in a mostly windowless apartment in Brooklyn with Jeff. We'd just failed our second attempt at regular parenthood but we were proud new puppy parents. Stella was three months old, and our apartment was overrun with toys and treats and pee pads. Jeff was working at Google, and I was working from home and contemplating going back to Google because my comedy career was going nowhere.

In early March, I was in the back seat of a Lyft on the Brooklyn-Queens Expressway on my way home from doing stand-up at Two Boots Pizza in Williamsburg when we were hit from behind by a truck and I was thrown from one side of the back seat to the other because I didn't have my seat belt on because I was too busy posting on Instagram about how I just performed at Two Boots Pizza. We veered across three lanes of traffic and it looked like we were about to be hit from all sides and I thought, *Oh my god. This is it. I'm going to die. I'll never see Stella again. And all because I just had to post a picture of me doing stand-up at Two Boots Pizza.* My obituary would have said, "Sarah Cooper (Two Boots Pizza) died today."

Thankfully, the driver pulled over safely and I wasn't really hurt, but I went to the hospital just in case. I ended up taking another

Lyft home from my Lyft accident. I followed up my Two Boots Pizza post with a picture of me in a neck brace to warn others about wearing their seat belts, and also to get some likes. Like a lot of you, I had spent the better part of the last four years pretty glued to social media, rage reading and doom scrolling.

I was addicted to social media. I was addicted to Twitter. That stupid app I saw demoed in 2007 was now all that was keeping me alive. For almost four years, I had been watching everything Trump did with despair and sick fascination. And I gotta be honest, I was reeeeally starting to regret voting for the guy.

The thing that I hated most about Trump (among the actual reasons) was that he was exactly the kind of president I'd be. I would be like, *how could he not read his intelligence briefings?* But the thing is, I've never shown up prepared to a meeting in my life. I'd get so mad he spent all morning in bed tweeting and watching TV, but I was also in bed all morning tweeting and watching TV. I love McDonald's. I heard he once had the Secret Service get him McDonald's in the middle of the night and I've done that, too, with Uber Eats. Uber Eats was my Secret Service. I love hotels and my steak well done. We both have degrees in economics, but neither of us understands money, and we've both been photographed with toilet paper stuck to our shoe. I guess the difference is, if I was president, I would have at least made an attempt to hide all that. Maybe that's where I went wrong in life.

When the world shut down, Jeff, Stella, and I were all stuck at home, like everyone else. Two Boots Pizza was closed and there were no shows or open mics, so I poured all my energy into making stuff for my first love: the internet. And a few weeks later I found my muse.

During one of his early COVID press conferences, Trump said, "We're gonna form a committee. I'm gonna call it a committee. And we're gonna make decisions. And we're gonna make decisions fairly quickly. And I hope they're going to be the right decisions."

Dude made it sound like he invented committees. And everyone around him nodded like it made sense. It seemed like everyone supported this nonsense and maybe I was the one who was out to lunch. The whole administration was a charade. It was Gaslighting 101. No, no, it was Advanced Gaslighting. He was pulling off being president with smoke and mirrors.

I decided to lip-synch it on this new app my nephews Ryan and Tyler showed me, called TikTok. Trump offered me the chance to be the ultimate tech bro. I wasn't trying to be Trump. I was trying to be the me I never got to be. The me I always wanted to be. The schmoozer. The guy who used a bunch of words but said nothing and got away with it. What a dream it would be to get away with something! Anything!

That first video was so much to fun to make but it didn't go viral. And I'm the type of person who moves on quickly to the next thing. I stopped watching his press conferences. They were unbearable anyway. But on April 23rd, Jeff came out of his office and said, "Sarah, you gotta see this." Trump had given a press conference—a press conference that would go on to live in Lysol infamy, where he said:

> *We hit the body, with a tremendous, whether it's ultraviolet or just a very powerful light. And I think you said that hasn't been checked, but you're gonna test it? And then I said supposing we brought the light inside the body, which you can do, either through the skin or in some other way. And I think you said you're gonna test that too, sounds interesting. And then I see the disinfectant knocks it out, in a minute, one minute, and is there a way we can do something like that? By injection, inside, or almost a cleaning. Because you see it gets in the lungs and it does a tremendous number on the lungs so it'd be interesting to check that, so that you're gonna have to use, medical doctors, right? But it sounds, it sounds interesting to me.*

I had no notes. It was a perfect clip. He was *so earnest*. He genuinely thought what he was saying *made sense*. And I wanted to become this man, the man that *I* saw, this man who had absolutely no idea how he sounded, who clearly saw himself as deeply intelligent and thoughtful. Here he was, humbly asking people to listen to his brilliant idea. To hit the body with a tremendous, whether it's ultraviolet or just a very powerful light. I mean, *Why wouldn't we do that? It just makes sense!* And then he mentions the doctors, but not just any doctors, the *medical* doctors.

I threw on a navy-blue blazer and got to work, in the living room, in the kitchen kneeling next to the sink, and back to the living room, just using whatever was around. I took off the blazer and put in clip-in bangs to create the version of myself that was listening to this nonsense and shot that, too. I did it all very quickly. I was rushing through it because I just wanted to get it over with—dinner was almost ready. My inner monologue while doing it was not, *Wow, this is hysterical,* it was, *Does this even make sense? Why am I doing this? No one is going to watch this.*

I spent two hours on the clip, shared it on my TikTok, and then shared it on Twitter. I chose the name "How to Medical" because I wanted some kind of broken sentence that didn't make sense and that's just what came out. And then we ate dinner. I'm pretty sure it

was jambalaya. I checked Twitter and saw that the video had a few retweets and a few comments, but just as I suspected, it wasn't going to go viral. I almost deleted it. But then I went to bed.

When I woke up, the video had a million views.

Earlier that week, a couple in Detroit, who were both essential workers, lost their only daughter to COVID. She was the youngest casualty thus far. I replied to my "How to Medical" tweet to encourage people to donate to her family and that reply started going viral, too. The attention was exciting, but feeling like it could actually help someone was even better.

I got a call from TMZ. They wanted to interview me. I got on the Zoom. They wanted to know how the video had changed my life, I said it hadn't. The interview never aired. Jerry Seinfeld mentioned me in *The New York Times*, but when I told my new stand-up comedy manager, Chris Burns, he said something like, "Your friends and family must be so excited."

So that was it. I went back to my unchanged life. I was going to find something else to do.

But Trump kept making these wild statements. And they were getting wilder and wilder. I didn't *want* to keep lip-synching, but it's like he was begging for it. And I did have a special set of skills that I'd been honing since I began singing (lip-synching) in church.

It didn't take long before I'd created a whole series. "How to Obamagate," "How to More Cases Than Anybody in the World," "How to Bible," "How to Lobster," "How to Very Positively," "How to Bunker," "How to Mask," "How to Empty Seat," and my pièce de résistance, "How to Person Woman Man Camera TV." This one took a solid 12 hours. He was so repetitive. It was so confusing. I kept trying to get it in one take and I was so frustrated with myself. I can't believe I came to the point where the perfectionist in me was overthinking and obsessing over a TikTok video. But I think the repetition is what helped me find things, each time I did a take, I found some new sniff, some new glance, some new idea for a prop.

Jeff brought me McDonald's. I like to think the Donald and I were both having McDonald's when I posted that final video.

People always ask me how I chose the clips. Man, the clips just chose themselves. I mean, who talks about lobsters like that? Who would answer the question "Are you a New Testament guy or an Old Testament guy?" with *"Uh, probably equal"*? Who would brag about being able to remember "person woman man camera TV" in their cognitive test, and then start to forget those same five words as they went on bragging about it? Who would loudly and proudly proclaim that "MAGA loves the Black people"? Only this guy.

Someone called my videos an antidote to the gaslighting, and that's what it felt like for me, too. Finally, we had some proof, some hilarious proof, that his words meant nothing.

Ryan Carroll Nelson

I got emails and drawings (like the one opposite from artist Ryan Carroll Nelson, @RyanCarrollNelson on Instagram) and letters from so many of you saying that I made you laugh when you didn't have anything else to laugh about. Emails like this one, shared with permission:

NAME: Candis McGovern

SUBJECT: Thank you

MESSAGE: My best friend's mom died of COVID-19 tonight. She went into the hospital 2 weeks ago with symptoms and never came out. She died alone and my best friend is grieving with her family and I'm insane with grief because I lost my mom when I was a teenager. I can't even hug my friend. They couldn't hug their mom. The reason that I'm telling you this is that your "how to wear a mask" video is the first thing that I've laughed at when I really thought I might never laugh again. Your work is indescribably important. Thank you so much for what you do.

I felt like I had made some kind of difference. Knowing I'd made someone smile when it was hard to smile made me feel proud. And I was no longer hiding behind an anonymous blog. People knew my name and my face. And that was pretty cool.

Each video I made got millions of views . . . then my life did start to change.

I started getting attention from all kinds of journalists and celebrities and people I'd always admired. Ben Stiller was commenting on my videos. Cher retweeted me. Halle Berry called me "iconic." I went from 60,000 Twitter followers to two million. I was on *Ellen*. I had an interview with Lawrence O'Donnell. And Nicolle Wallace. Jimmy Fallon had me on *The Tonight Show*. Kamala Harris wanted to do an Instagram Live with me.

Kamala Harris. My parents said we were probably related!

And suddenly, very suddenly, like so fast it'll make your head spin, and my head was spinning, I was pretty much handed the keys to Hollywood.

I signed with WME and they quickly made so many dreams come true. I started auditioning for high-profile projects. I got offered a series regular role on a sitcom. One day I'm at the park with Stella and I get a text from Ricky Gervais. We sold a pilot for *100 Tricks to Appear Smart in Meetings* to Netflix and I'd be working with Ricky Gervais. *Ricky Gervais.* We sold another pilot for *How to Be Successful Without Hurting Men's Feelings* to CBS with Nina Tassler and Cindy Chupack. My manager texted me and said they want me to guest-host *Kimmel*. HOST. *KIMMEL.* I met with Natasha Lyonne and Maya Rudolph and they wanted to work with me on a Netflix comedy special. I was getting a Netflix comedy special.

And then I was like, wow, I'm really glad I voted for him. Just to be clear, I did not vote for him.

If this feels fast to you, it felt that way to me, too. I can't describe the imposter syndrome that engulfed me as all this was happening. It engulfs me even now as I write this. I'm getting imposter syndrome writing my own memoir.

I started getting recognized on the street.

The first time I got recognized I was picking up dog poop, because when you get famous for lip-synching Donald Trump, that's the only thing that makes sense. I was walking Stella and she had just done her business like a good girl. I bent down to pick up the poop but I couldn't open the green poop bag. So I pull down my mask to lick my fingers to open the bag during a global pandemic, and as I'm scooping this poop, I hear, "Are you Sarah Cooper?"

I look up midscoop and see this blond girl, about 12 years old, looking down at me. And I'm like, *Oh my god, it's happening! It's finally happening.* I laughed and smiled and said, "Yes, I'm Sarah Cooper!" And then I wanted to make conversation because I've never been recognized before and of course I want my fans to love me, so I said, "Are you on TikTok?"

And she goes, "No . . . my dad sends me your videos."

Cool, cool, I thought.

"Cool," I said out loud.

Stella saw the whole thing. I was so embarrassed. I'd become an email forward from someone's dad.

Dads love my videos. And I love dads. But I had to confront the fact that I'd built my whole life on dad humor. I know what you're thinking: *That was just one person* (that's what you were thinking, right?), but people came up to me all the time to say their dad loved my videos. In fact, two months later I was shooting my Netflix special and Marisa Tomei came over to me and said, "Sarah! Sarah! Can I get a picture with you?" I was floored. I was like, "Oh my god, Marisa Tomei wants a picture with me?" And she said, "No, it's for my dad."

All of this newfound recognizability was hard on my relationship with Jeff.

At one point he said, "I'm scared you're gonna get famous and leave me."

And I said, "I'm not gonna get famous."

He wanted us to go back to couples counseling. He found someone who would meet with us over Zoom, and during our first session, we say our hellos and introductions and the next thing the therapist says is, "Wait, are you Sarah Cooper?"

Over the next few years, so many people recognized me, always with kind words. People come up to me and say, "I love you," or "Thank you," or tell me I kept them sane during the pandemic. And, yes, sometimes they mention their dad. And usually I say that making those videos kept me sane, too. But it wasn't making them, it was seeing how happy they made other people. That's what kept me sane.

Many, many, many months later, there was a time I became sort of embarrassed of the videos, like I didn't want to be associated with Trump. I didn't want to just be known for lip-synching. I didn't want the push notification from TMZ about my death to say, "This Trump impersonator died: Click to find out how." But that's my imposter syndrome talking, trying to undermine what these videos actually meant.

These videos weren't really about Trump. They were about my (our) frustration with a culture of entitlement and bullshit that valued the egos of rich (white) men over accountability.

And I'm not just saying that because I read it in this article by James Poniewozik for *The New York Times*:

> *She captures her Trump entirely through pantomime. She crosses her arms and bounces on her heels, like a C.E.O. filibustering through a meeting while the staff suffers. Plenty of wags seized on Mr. Trump's bleach prescription for easy jokes, but her performance gets at something deeper: the peacocky entitlement of the longtime boss who is used to having his every whim indulged, his every thought-doodle praised as a Michelangelo.*

Look at me seamlessly inserting good press into my memoir.

A reporter once asked Trump if he'd seen my videos and he said he hadn't but in a way that made me think he definitely had.

People keep asking me to do Trump again and I never will. I just find him so boring now. We've seen that he's a little man behind a curtain. But he did teach me that there's something to be said for faking it until you make it. If he can walk around with that kind of confidence, why can't we?

Like the confidence to believe that someone would pay $15,000 to talk to you on Zoom.

Indeed, at one point in the whirlwind, the great Sir Jake Tapper asked me to donate a 30-minute Zoom conference call to the Homes For Our Troops charity auction. And someone really bid

$15,000 to talk to me on Zoom. I was shocked and flattered. And excited. But that excitement turned to confusion when eight long and quiet months passed before the winner reached out to schedule their "prize." I guess they had a lot going on.

When the Zoom finally connected, I found myself face-to-face with a young woman. And I was like, *Oh wow, a young woman wants to chat with me!* This was exactly the demographic I was after. But the first thing she said to me was, "Wow, you look really tired." I was rightfully taken quite aback. *Is that how you speak to your . . . hero?* I thought. I was hurt and embarrassed and embarrassed about how hurt I was, which naturally transformed into a passive-aggressive rage.

"Yeah, sorry, I'm going through a divorce. I've been living out of a suitcase for two months. Also, it's a pandemic, it's kind of a hard time for a lot of people."

She was so apologetic: "Oh, I'm sorry, I'm sorry!" And I laughed and told her it was okay. I decided that maybe she just had really bad social skills. But then I thought, *If her social skills are this bad, where did she get $15,000 for a Zoom call from?*

I asked her what she wanted to talk about. We were down to 28 minutes and 42 seconds.

She pulled out a sheet of paper with printed questions and she started reading off it.

"What is your next project in development and where did you learn acting school?"

It was a generic and boring question and she asked it in a generic and boring way. She was bored. I could tell she didn't want to be on this call. At all. *Maybe it's just really boring to be someone who has $15,000 for a Zoom call?* I got nervous. I was expecting a superfan.

After three more bored questions, I finally asked her, "Did you come up with these questions?"

"No," she admitted.

"Do you know who I am?" I asked.

"Not really," she laughed.

I was bewildered and confused. I had to know.

"Did you buy this Zoom call?"

She hesitated.

"No. It was a gift from my dad."

It's So Nice to Be in Hell

LET'S SEE. What else happened in 2020?

Oh yeah, I shot a Netflix special with Helen Mirren. I did a lip-synching scene with her. She rehearsed with me over and over again and was so fun and patient and so game for anything. She made me feel like we were old friends. In fact, I felt so close to her that after we shot that scene, I went up to her and I said, "We should do Shakespeare together."

To Academy Award–winning actress Helen Mirren, I said, "We should do Shakespeare together."

So you can see why I sometimes have thoughts like, *I should not be out in public, I should stay inside and never leave and never talk to anyone ever. I can't be trusted.*

Maya Rudolph was my executive producer. I said words to her. Many words.

Natasha Lyonne directed my special. She'd come over and say, "Sarah, that was great, but this time can you maybe try anything else? Just, like, literally, anything else."

I won't list everyone I worked with on *Sarah Cooper: Everything's Fine*, because that would be obnoxious, and you can go to Netflix for that. But just know I worked with them all in the span of eight days. NO HUMAN PERSON SHOULD MEET ALL OF THEIR HEROES IN EIGHT DAYS. It's just not safe. I had no time to process it.

My cinematographer was Polly Morgan. Watching her work with Natasha on set was a MasterClass in creative collaboration, a real-life, in-the-flesh, whirlwind MasterClass.

It took almost 100 filmmakers to pull this off, from lighting to sound, to visual effects, to camera, to art and graphic design, to transportation. Trayce Gigi Field was a genius with costumes and put together over 50 looks even though many stores weren't open. Jason Orion, Mary Daniels, and Annette Chaisson created hair and makeup for me and our 20 cast members in full hazmat suits.

Here's where you stop reading, go to Netflix, watch my special, and pause on the credits. Because each of those people is so good at what they do, and welcomed me into this world, this world I've wanted to be in my whole life. And they did it with smiles behind their masks while having to put up with a TikTok star who had no idea what she was doing.

But who was also somehow their boss.

I did it. I became a clueless boss!

Everything about this project was meta like that—I felt like I was falling apart, and we were creating a show about the world falling apart, and the world felt like it was *actually* falling apart, too. We were six months into a two-week quarantine. The election was coming up. We had barely survived the last four years and we couldn't take four more. There was an urgency to what we were doing. It felt like we all wanted to shake this feeling of powerlessness and bring some joy into people's lives.

My first meeting with Maya, Natasha, and Danielle Renfrew Behrens of Animal Pictures was on June 19, 2020. Our special premiered on October 27. It was fast. I was not prepared. But I pretended to be prepared, I pretended pretty hard. I finally understood the feeling Tina Fey dubbed "blorft": "completely overwhelmed but proceeding as if everything is fine and reacting to the stress with the torpor of a possum."

We put a pitch deck together in days. During our first few meetings, we came up with this concept of a news anchor having to keep it together while the world self-destructs, inspired by that great KC Green illustration of a dog sipping tea in an inferno. That's what this super-funny comedy special was going to be about: disassociation. I love *Mr. Show* and I wanted to create sketches that seamlessly wove in and out of each other. Natasha was excited to visually represent a descent into madness. By the end of the week, Maya had already written the *Everything's Fine* theme song. And Danielle joked, "We need to be picture locked yesterday." And I was like, "What's picture locked?"

My manager, Chris Burns, and my agents at WME, Allysa Mahler and Mike Berkowitz, sent the deck out to Netflix, HBO, HBO Max, Netflix, FX, Comedy Central / Viacom, Amazon, Apple, Peacock, Hulu, and Netflix. But it all seemed like a formality. Netflix was on board almost immediately and became the most supportive partner. We did seem destined to work together. We both got our start in tech. We both tried to win it in the tech game, but our hearts were always in entertainment. After a brief meeting with Netflix, it was done. We were making a special. At the time, I had no idea how anything worked so I just assumed this is how it always worked. But now I know, this is not at all how anything usually works.

I flew out to LA. We had six shoot days plus two pre-shoot shoot days. It was a tight, tight schedule. You could not fit a vibrator into this schedule. Animal Pictures and Alex Bach and Dan Powell at Irony Point pulled off a miracle. On top of everything, this special would be the first time most of the cast and crew had worked again since being in lockdown, so we had to figure out how to keep everyone safe.

Meanwhile, I was moving into an Airbnb with Jeff and Stella. My life got turned upside down and it was unsurprisingly putting a strain on our relationship. Not my relationship with Stella, that was fine. My relationship with Jeff. He was very supportive of the success I was having but it was all a shock for both of us. I was on the phone with Natasha freakin' Lyonne for hours on end, which felt totally normal but utterly surreal at the same time. Jeff was worried I was treating him differently. And the truth is, I had to. For eight years, he had been my number one priority, but now I had legit other shit to do. And it was hard not to sound uppity when saying things like, "I can't talk now, I have a Zoom rehearsal with Dame Helen Mirren." (She demanded we always refer to her as Dame Helen Mirren.)

To offset my lack of availability, I felt like I needed to tone down how monumental this all was for me and act like it wasn't a big deal, when it was literally the biggest deal of all the deals that I have ever dealt with.

The writers' room was led by Paula Pell. I KNOW. Natasha, Maya, Danielle, and Chris pulled together the funniest writer submission packets I'd ever read. We hired Jasmine Pierce, Jordan Black, Cole Escola, Jocelyn Richard, Jake Fogelnest, Katie Morrissey, Charlie Sanders, and Lizzie Rose. Within a day, Paula and Cole had created the character of KJ Dillard, maker of Cupcake Shoes, who would eventually be played by Jane Lynch, and a Ken Burns–style parody of the history of Karens that would go on to be narrated by Whoopi Goldberg.

I KNOW.

We had our first writers' room table read. It didn't go so well. Table reads scare the shit out of me and I'm the queen of bombing them. Natasha and I talked after. She asked me if I'd rather do a straight stand-up special with a socially distanced audience. And I said no. I might've been high. I was under so much pressure. I said yes to as much as I could fit on my plate. And I'm glad I did. It was a lot and I was just blorft enough to believe I could handle it. Make a sketch special. No problem. The truth is, if it weren't for Natasha, it never would have come together. Her ambition inspired me. She's the kind of person who's either making something or thinking about making something 24 hours a day.

I'm glad I didn't do a stand-up special, because I never would have gotten to see Aubrey Plaza play the most ludicrous QVC host in history, in this sketch Natasha and I wrote in the middle of the night.

ASHLEY
It's the three a.m. hour here on QAnon QVC.
And yes, this is the real QAnon, not the
other one people were saying was the real
one on 4chan. Please stop doxing me. I've
had to move five times.
(then)
Let's check in with our viewers. "Emma" from
Philadelphia! How are you this morning?

EMMA FROM PHILADELPHIA
Hey Ashley, longtime caller, always
listening. You blinked your right eye last
night when you were selling jewelry. Was
that a sign that you have been contacted by
the God of Fire?

ASHLEY
Don't be ridiculous, "Emma," which I know
is not your real name. That was simply a
nervous tic in my eye. It wasn't a secret
coded message. Believe me, you'll KNOW when
I've been contacted by the God of Fire!

In addition to executive producing and writing and composing and singing, Maya took on the role of Andrea Steele, a meteorologist at the end of her weather-balloon rope. The Maya Day, as it was forever known, was the most I laughed on set. She makes it look easy. I know what you're thinking: Sarah, she's Maya Rudolph, of course she does. But to see it up close was stunning, which is why I look so stunned in that sketch, written by Jasmine Pierce.

                    ANDREA
AM I OKAY?! This bitch. AM I OKAY?! Um, no,
no I don't think I AM OK actually! We got a
bat disease just floating around in the sky!
There's a new natural disaster every day!
Factories destroying the environment! Look
at this got-damn forecast! We all know
what's causing this deadass BULLSHIT. You
want to get me started on climate change?
Really? You know this shit already! I don't
need to tell you! This is the first time I've
left my house in months! All it takes is one
wrong motherfucker to breathe on me funny.

                    SARAH
Uh, Scooter, we're still on a nine-second
delay, right?

                    SCOOTER
                  (smiling)
Oh no, the woman who pushes that button
stopped coming in weeks ago.

Jasmine also wrote a sketch we unfortunately didn't have time
to shoot. It was a parody of a Sarah McLachlan SPCA commercial,
asking for donations to billionaires:

                    SARAH
Hi, I'm Sarah Cooplachlan. And for just
sixty thousand dollars a month, you can
help support a billionaire in need. That's
just one Manhattan rent per day. That's
just seventeen cups of coffee an hour. Most
billionaires don't know where their next
paycheck is coming from. Because they have
too many sources of passive income. It's
hard to keep track.

When we first started talking about the set, I offered to bring my green screen cloth over to LA, just so you know where my head was at. Walking into both sets, designed by JC Molina and Sofia Midon, left me speechless.

The control room was an idea I had early in the process. I see now I was trying to bring to life this negative voice in my head. I always kind of imagine there's a producer in a control room constantly judging me and listing my flaws through my headset, except they aren't as funny as Eddie Pepitone and Marcella Arguello.

The tough part was taking those lip-synching videos and shooting them at this scale. Stuff that I did off-the-cuff at home now had to be scripted and planned. And lip-synching on a golf course in front of a hundred people was very different from doing it at home alone on my iPhone. I was nervous, there was pressure, I was trying way too hard. But thank god for editing. The result was something new and different on its own. But don't just take my word for it, go watch it. See how funny Connie Chung is. She was nervous, she wasn't sure she could do comedy, turns out she's Carol Burnett. I still can't believe I got to write a sketch about AI taking over CEOs' jobs, with a little nod to *The Naked Gun* in there as well, starring the most sensually funny man on earth: Ben Stiller. Watch him as Robot CEO "massage" my shoulders. It's probably my favorite part. And we did that at two different times with video feeds; we were never in the same room. I have to thank our editors for that and so much else. And behold Fred Armisen. A man who can make you laugh with a look. He looks at you and you laugh. You can't help it. And Jordan Black. He was one of our writers and Natasha put him into a few of the sketches, and thank god. He stole every scene.

I was exactly where I wanted to be, but I felt pretty disconnected from myself. I finally understood *The Little Mermaid* song "Part of Your World." You want to be where the people are, whichever people you want to be, you want to be with them. And you feel like an outsider. Like you'll never be there. And then you get there, and you have no voice! Every day I had to make a hundred tiny decisions based on my gut, but my gut was pretty buried. Natasha and Polly and Maya collaborated with these distinct, creative instincts, but I wasn't used to collaborating, I was used to being an individual contributor. Thank god I was surrounded by people who are way funnier and smarter than me.

On the last day of filming, I got my temperature checked, as I did every day, but for the first time I had a fever. I panicked. I thought, *This is it, this is how it all falls apart.* They took my temperature again and it turned out I had just been standing in the fire sun too long. Oh yeah, there were raging fires that made the air toxic to breathe. We couldn't be inside too long because of COVID but we couldn't be outside too long because of the air quality. *I could make a* Sophie's Choice *joke here but I won't.*

I FLEW BACK TO NEW YORK and a few weeks later Netflix sent me the link to watch *Sarah Cooper: Everything's Fine* for the first time. Jeff held my hand. The music swells. We hear the voice of Tom Kane—"This is Sarah Cooper"—and it's a thrill. When you're in the middle of it, it's so hard to picture the final product. You start to second-guess every decision. But Jeff and I watched it and we laughed.

And now I watch it every night alone. Just kidding. But I did watch it a few weeks ago to write this chapter. It's so hard to watch myself, and it took me a full 30 minutes to press play. But once I did, I was overwhelmed with how visually stunning it is. After having been "in the industry" for three years, I have no idea how this even got made and no idea how it is so good.·

At the end of the special, Fred sings a song called "It's So Nice to Be in Hell." Oh yeah, Fred Armisen wanted to "help out," so on top of playing Scooter, he wrote the parking-lot magician sketch, AND wrote and performed the closing song, no big deal. And it's such a brilliant ending. It's the opposite of saying everything's fine. It's

admitting we're in hell and accepting it, which is really the only way through it.

Charmaine came into town to see our billboard in Times Square on the same day the 2020 election was called for Joe Biden. I hadn't reentered my body yet when I took this picture of us, but when I look at it now, I just think, *Wow. That really happened.*

If I learned anything, and I did learn a lot, it's that two things can be true at the same time.

You can love Jon Hamm. You could've watched every episode of *Mad Men* six times. You can crack up every time he says "pilluhs" as Steve Windell (in a brilliant sketch written by Jocelyn Richard). And you can still stand next to him on set for an entire hour and not say a single word.

You can feel scared and worried and utterly humiliated, and you can love every minute of it.

You can be in hell, and it can still be pretty nice.

I Heard You're Killing It

MY FIRST MEETING WITH MR. SEINFELD was an unexpected one. I ran into him at a Netflix comedy luncheon a few weeks after I accepted the role of Poppy Northcutt in his film *Unfrosted*. I was there alone and felt a bit out of place but then thankfully I saw Tig Notaro, who I love. I met her in 2020 when I did her podcast and then we did Just For Laughs together, but now I finally got to meet her in person. I sat at her table, relieved and ready to get drunk on mimosas. But then I saw Jerry Seinfeld. I panicked a bit. I felt like I wasn't prepared to meet him. I hadn't meditated that day. I wasn't in the game, I wasn't focused, I didn't have on sunscreen. I forgot my inhaler. I don't use an inhaler. I hid behind a waiter. But it was too late.

As soon as Jerry saw me, he came over and shook my hand and thanked me for doing the movie. I thanked him right back. He told me how he thought my videos really held up, they were still funny. And I wanted to say that's exactly how I felt about *Seinfeld*, that even when I knew exactly what was coming, I still laughed. But instead I did the best thing you can ever do as a comedian to another comedian—I started doing a bit. Yup, I started doing a bit. I told him dads love my videos. Yeah, you know that material about dads loving my videos from two chapters ago? I started doing that. In my head I'm like, *Sarah you're doing a bit, stop, stop doing a bit, oh god just get to the punch line, no no no abort now! Abort! Abort! But we can't abort without doing the punch line? Then he'll think we aren't funny? He already thinks you're not funny, you're trying to work a bit into regular conversation! Top lip, bottom lip, together, NOW.* I stopped talking. Jerry laughed politely (thankfully he's not stingy with a polite laugh), and before I knew it, he was walking away. And I watched him stop to talk to Tig Notaro. And he was cracking up. He was literally bent over, dying laughing talking to Tig Notaro. God, I hate Tig Notaro.

Look, it's the end of the book. You know me pretty well by now. You've seen me interact with all kinds of people, celebrities included, and I've been cool, I've been chill, I've been downright professional. But we all have that one person who if we met them in person it would throw us off balance and make us reveal the most neurotic versions of ourselves. Maybe for you that's Oprah or Obama. For me, it was Jerry Seinfeld.

I wasn't always a fan of *Seinfeld*. When *Seinfeld* was new on TV every week I hated *Seinfeld*. Because everyone was talking about *Seinfeld*. And it was annoying and cliché and I wasn't going to concern myself with this lowest-common-denominator drivel. But sometime in my late twenties I watched an episode of *Seinfeld* called "The Marine Biologist," and when George pulled that golf ball out of his jacket I thought it was the single greatest moment in TV history. I marveled at how it was surprising but also made complete sense. It was godlike writing. Later, there was a solid four years where I fell asleep to *Seinfeld* reruns every night. Most shows are all setup, but *Seinfeld* was all punch lines. Even the setups were punch lines. I studied it. I wanted to make something like that. I still do. I wanted to do what he did, go from open mics, to a late-night set, to a hit TV show, and then, bada bing, bada boom, billionaire.

Right before the pandemic hit, I was considering getting a full-time job because I was nowhere near being a bada-bing billionaire. And I was on the phone talking to my mom about it and she suggested I get on *Comedians in Cars Getting Coffee*. The reason she suggested that was because, in her words, "maybe it pays." As if I could just get on a show like that, and as if the only reason to do it would be because *maybe it pays*. I went to an open mic that night and shared that onstage; it got a laugh.

The point is, I never thought in a million years I would ever work with, or meet, or talk to, or have a Zoom with, or even have myself exist as a thought in the mind of Jerry Seinfeld. So when he shared my "How to Medical" clip, it was huge. And when I got this part in his movie, it was seismic. And I never use that word.

Before filming began, Jerry was kind enough to set up a rehearsal for us. And I didn't do much to prepare, just met with a few acting coaches, rehearsed with a friend, repeated the lines in my head at any moment of rest, rehearsed with another friend, blocked the scenes in different shoe options, and set up an extra therapy session. I told my therapist how nervous I was. And how bad I felt about doing a bit when I first met Jerry. I told her I really wanted to have an actual conversation with him. And my therapist told me to tell him what a superfan I am. And it made sense to me. *Be genuine,* I thought. Yeah. Be honest. Tell him everything. He will love it. He will LOVE it.

So I show up to rehearsal and Jerry was wearing a white shirt and I was wearing a white blazer, and I thought that was a good sign (it wasn't). We discuss the script. He says, "It's easy to make someone care about something important, but to get someone to care about something as dumb as a Pop-Tart, well, that takes special skill." And with my signature wit I volleyed back, "That's so true."

I walked into his office. He sat on the couch. I sat on the chair in front of the desk, which was facing away from the couch. And instead of turning the chair to talk to him, I awkwardly turned only my upper body to face him, while still keeping my lower body facing the desk. I tried to make it look casual. *Yeah. Real casual, Sarah. Look how cool you look with your body twisted in half.* And Jerry notices and suggests I turn the chair around and be comfortable. Comfortable. Right.

Then I proceed to follow my therapist's advice. I tell Jerry what a big fan I am, how I binge-watch *Seinfeld*, how I believe him sharing "How to Medical" is what sparked all my success, how he's the reason I was able to get a divorce and be on my own as an independent woman, how my mom suggested I get on *Comedians in Cars Getting Coffee* because "maybe it pays." And without missing a beat, he goes, "It does pay." Hmm. Maybe doing material was a better idea.

The following week, filming began. Everything seemed so perfect. I was in a hotel room with a perfect view of the Hollywood sign. Gaston Pierre picked me up to drive me to set, a fellow Jamaican. When I got there, I was greeted by Yani Gutierrez, who PA'd my comedy special.

Not to mention the fact that I was doing a movie with the humor of *Seinfeld* and the look of *Mad Men* and it was about CEREAL. It was a dream I didn't even know I had. I loved my character, I loved the cast, I loved the crew, I loved the sets. I could not believe the wardrobe. Susan Matheson was meticulous. My bob wig was made just for me by Teressa Hill, based on magazine clippings and a picture I sent her of my mom in the 1960s. And my makeup! Denise Paulson and Bill Corso. I have never looked cuter in my life.

During that first week I met Adrian Martinez. What a guy. You instantly feel like his friend. And so talented. He got an applause break on set after doing just one line. He took risks, he was fearless, it was amazing.

The following week, Jim Gaffigan shows up. In 2014, he popped into Gotham Comedy Club on the night I was doing a bringer with eight of my Google coworkers, and he totally kills, and I had to go on right after him and it sucked. And now I get to be on set with him and he's so charming and generous and I cannot believe my life.

On set, Jerry would go from directing to writing to acting to writing back to directing back to acting and he was the same guy no matter what he was doing. He was the same guy in rehearsal as he was on set as he was on camera as he was on *Seinfeld* as he was in his specials as he was in a TV interview 20 years ago. Utterly seamless. Me? I don't even know who I am as I write this.

And Jerry was so chill. One time a crew member got a little heated and the set got anxious and quiet, and Jerry immediately jumps in: "Alright, let's just calm down, keep it calm, remember: We're making a movie about a Pop-Tart." And his voice kinda squeaks on the "pop" part and everyone laughs. The mood is light again, instantly. And I *saw something*. Power isn't yelling and cursing, it's shifting the mood of 200 people from fear to relaxation with seven words. We're making a movie about a Pop-Tart. That's power.

And with great power comes . . . great . . . confusing feelings.

Now, here's the part that's especially hard to admit. I convinced myself I was in love with Jerry Seinfeld.

Note here for Jessica Seinfeld (who I have never met but she was kind enough to send me a copy of her Vegan, at Times *cookbook, now available wherever books are sold): I am not now, nor was I ever, in love with your husband. According to my therapist, I was doing something close to hallucinating, and she is happy to share with you her notes from those sessions.*

But yes, I convinced myself I was in love with him. He was my boss in the movie and my boss in real life, not to mention this mythical icon I'd worshipped for decades. I dare you not to confuse that with love. And now the true humiliation begins.

I started listening to the car podcast of the film's cowriter, Spike Feresten, called *Spike's Car Radio* on Apple Podcasts, where Jerry was sometimes a guest. I hate driving. I don't own a car. I can't stand white guys with podcasts. But I became addicted to this podcast. There was one episode where a neighbor's dog wandered over to where they were recording and I heard

Jerry talk to the dog and it did seem like a slightly different Jerry voice than I'd heard before and I thought it was so cute.

I created a playlist of songs that were popular when Jerry was 30. I thought this would help me get inside his mind. Back in my hotel room, I'd turn out the lights and point this starry light projector at the ceiling and dance to "Listen to the Music" by the Doobie Brothers over and over again. I was 44 years old.

I decided that Jerry and I were destined to be in a romantic comedy together. I started writing the script. The imaginary soundtrack might have included the Doobie Brothers. I called my friend Katie (who has a full-time job) *and made her rehearse the script with me.*

I

LOST

MY

MIND.

But don't worry, friends, don't worry. I quickly regained control of the situation. After a few weeks, I realized I was not, in fact, in love with Jerry Seinfeld. No. I was just a superfan. I realized how misguided this teenage girl devotion was. I became a completely sane human being again. I stopped listening to the podcast (mostly, I mean, it is a good podcast). I shelved the romantic comedy (unless someone wants to option it). And I reduced my Doobie Brothers intake to once or twice a week. And with this newfound sense of maturity, self-awareness, and growth, I thought, *You know what? You know what Sarah's gonna do? You know what super-smart, super-chill Sarah's gonna do? Sarah's gonna be Jerry Seinfeld's friend.*

So I journaled: How could I be Jerry Seinfeld's friend? How could I prove to him once and for all that I am a normal human being? And I realized the way to do that was to give him a compliment. Yeah, that's the ticket. Normal people give compliments, that's a normal person thing to do. I was gonna give him an adult professional compliment on the set of an adult professional film. Not an adult film. I mean, you know what I mean. It's fine. We're all fine here.

I brainstormed: What compliment could I give him? What would make me feel good if someone said it to me on a movie set? It had to be something he hadn't heard before. Yeah, a compliment Jerry Seinfeld has never received. A man who has literally received every compliment anyone could possibly receive was about to get a compliment from me that would top every other compliment he's ever gotten.

Finally, I flowcharted: I had to get it right. I knew I'd only get one shot at this.

And after a few days of journaling and brainstorming and flowcharting, I came up with the perfect compliment. The compliment to end all compliments. I was going to say (to Jerry Seinfeld): I heard you're killing it.

You read that right.

I heard you're killing it.

It was foolproof.

The next day we were between takes. Jerry came over to where I was sitting, and I thought, *This is my moment to give him the compliment.*

So I look up at Jerry Seinfeld (writer, director, and star of the film) and I say, "Hey, I heard you're killing it."

And without missing a beat he goes, "Who said that?"

And after missing several beats, I say . . . "Uh, people?"

"That was a good compliment right up until the end there," he said. And he walked away. And I watched him stop to talk to Adrian Martinez. And Adrian had Jerry doubled over laughing, literally writhing on the concrete floor laughing. And I've said this before and I'll say it again, I cannot fucking stand Adrian Martinez. #BoycottAdrianMartinez.

There was a banquet scene where I got to sit in a fancy dress at a dinner table across from Jerry Seinfeld and Jim Gaffigan in tuxes. Jim said, "This whole business is someone telling you to come here, come here, come here, and then you come, and they slap you across the face." Then Jim Gaffigan made Jerry laugh so hard he couldn't breathe and I wanted to slap him across the face. Except I was laughing, too, that jerk.

Between takes, Jerry said something that stuck with me and, to be honest, kind of inspired the title of this book. He said, "This is the business of being embarrassed." When he said it, I realized I'd been running from embarrassment my whole life. And I was having such a hard time. I couldn't relax. I was so scared of being embarrassed and trying so hard to hide it.

The conversation moved on and I mentioned to Jim that I was 1 percent Ashkenazi Jew. Jerry turned and said, "Do you think that makes you part of the club? That doesn't make you part of the club!" He was joking. But he was also serious, I think. We were rolling again and Jerry took a sip of water and did a spit take around the table like a sprinkler and I laughed so hard I couldn't breathe.

A few weeks later it was over. My last scene was me dancing in the Kellogg's break room. And Jerry said he'd start the scene with me. And I asked him to stand on my right side because the left side of my face is my good side. And I wasn't trying to make a joke, I literally needed my left side to be facing the camera. And I swear to you, I swear on my life . . . I got a guffaw. I hadn't workshopped that bit at all.

Before heading back to New York, I took a selfie with Jerry and then used a filter on it to make it look like we were in a rainbow. Then I went to FedEx/Kinko's and printed it out and put it in a thank-you card using a glue stick. Then I gave him the card. Most of me hopes he didn't open it, and also here it is:

Anyway, thanks, Jer. Can I call you Jer? Thank you for the grace you showed me in my most humiliating moments. I'm lucky that a person as kind as you was my Oprah or Obama.

Epilogue

During the shoot, I was hanging out with Snap, Crackle, and Pop in a cemetery. And I decided to ask Crackle, played by Mikey Day, what he thought of the compliment I gave Jerry.

I said, "Hey, Mikey, can I ask you something?"

"Sure, what's up?" he said, because he's a sweetheart.

"What would you say if someone on this set came up to you and said, 'I heard you're killing it'?"

"'I heard you're killing it'?" he said.

"Yeah. 'I heard you're killing it.'"

Mikey thinks for a second, then says, "Well, first I'd say fuck off."

Oh god.

"Then I'd say, who said that?"

I gulped.

He asked me if I said that to someone on this set.

I nodded.

"Cast or crew?" he said.

I didn't want to say.

"Oh no, not cast?" he said. "Surely you didn't go straight to the top with that one?"

I looked down.

Surely, I did.

And don't call me Shirley.

Coop d'État

ONE NIGHT I WAS WALKING HOME and I saw a young woman crying on a sidewalk bench. She was wringing her hands and tears were streaming down her face. And I was going to just let her be, because I don't know any woman who hasn't cried in public. My go-to spots are Starbucks, Target, and the Starbucks inside the Target. I figured I'd keep on walking. But then I couldn't shake how sad she looked. I sat down next to her.

"Hi," I said. "Are you okay?"

"Wow, do I look that bad?" she said.

"No, you don't look bad! Just sad."

And she wiped her face and said, "I messed up at my job. And I'm just sitting here thinking about every mistake I've ever made."

And it was so weird hearing her say that, because I used to think about every mistake I've ever made all the time.

The woman stared at me.

"Oh, sorry," I said. "I was just gonna say, I used to think about every mistake I've ever made all the time."

"Really?" she said.

"Yeah."

She turned to me.

"What mistakes have you made?"

I clammed up. I didn't even know where to begin. I mean I did. But was I really gonna say it out loud?

I'm 45. I'm twice divorced. I got so many opportunities in the last three years and felt like I squandered them. So many auditions

I blew. So many amazing people I met but I didn't say the right things to. I went through a period of total fear. Wanting to hide. Waking up with thoughts like, *You suck, you're such a loser. Why'd you say that?* Inside my mind, a movie called *My Most Embarrassing Moments* played on repeat. And it was not yet a comedy. And speaking of comedies, the TV pilots for *100 Tricks to Appear Smart in Meetings* and *How to Be Successful without Hurting Men's Feelings* were both passed on, and I felt like a failure. I'd never worked harder on anything else in my life. I wondered if my only talent was lip-synching Donald Trump. That's not even a real talent. Could I really be that cursed? Maybe that wedding sand ceremony I did in Puerto Rico WAS a satanic ritual.

I thought about the last time I went to see Stella. Per the terms of our divorce, I have monthly visitation rights (supervised). I played with Stella and I started crying because I was so worried about the future. And Jeff gave me a little pep talk. He said, "You always figure it out, Sarah, it's gonna be okay." And he was so kind and made me feel so much better. And I realized he was part of my confidence. Being married made me feel like I was doing something right. Just like that burst of Hollywood success made me feel like I was doing something right. But I had to find that confidence on my own. Cue cheesy inspirational music.

I was always trying to be perfect and it was fucking exhausting. I was always taking heaven and turning it into hell. When was I ever going to stop?

"Ma'am, are you okay?" the woman asked me.

I was sick of the negative voice in my head. It's just as much of an authoritarian as a real authoritarian. Nothing is ever good enough or done fast enough. You have to try as hard as you can and do it perfectly and be the best and keep an eye on who's doing better than you and do it on your own and if you don't succeed, you're lazy. And the internet makes it worse. It's a comparison machine. It makes you think there *is* one right answer for everything. And I realized that's where all my anxiety came from: thinking there was one right answer in all situations and if I didn't get it right, I was a failure and I'd be punished. But there isn't one right answer. I mean, maybe there is if you're a scientist, but I'm not a scientist. I'm a writer!

And realizing that is what helped me finally overthrow that voice in my head, in a sort of . . . *coop d'état*, if you will. I replaced that voice with a more chill voice. A voice that says, *I did what I did. I said what I said. I'm right where I'm supposed to be.* I'm grateful for everything I got, even the slaps. Hell, I want to be slapped by Hollywood. Like, real good. I want to make a TV show, I want to write a fantasy novel, I want to direct. And it's all possible. After all, I *am* a 45-year-old woman who's been divorced twice. That's like three comedy specials right there.

Life is not a competition of power. It is a competition of knowing yourself. The better you know yourself, the more powerful you are. So, yeah, I guess it is a competition of power? Whatever, I'm not a thought leader! You can't get to know yourself without some trial and error or without allowing yourself to make a mistake. And the more foolish you are, the more mistakes you make, the more you learn about yourself and the more powerful you become. You know, within reason.

My dad was absolutely terrified of any of us failing. Because he was walking the tightrope he and all immigrants walk, feeling like one wrong move and it would all be over. That's not an environment conducive to taking chances. And that terror lives inside me, too, but my opportunity to take risks *is* my parents' legacy.

Yeah, it's exhausting trying to be a human being whose life doesn't look like everyone else's. Creating your own path is hard. Like if two paths forged in the wood and you didn't take the pristine one or the one less traveled by, I don't know, I don't really know poems. But you take neither path. Actually you take one of the paths, and you realize it's not for you and you grab a machete and . . . Wow, I think I finally understand "Welcome to the Jungle," by Guns N' Roses.

If you're out there thinking about every mistake you've ever made, don't. You did it exactly the way you were supposed to. Get excited about what you'll try next time, because there *will* be a next time.

Now that I'd said this to myself, I was finally ready to say all of this out loud to this woman, to lift her spirits and give her a guiding hand. I turned to her.

But when I started talking to her, I lost my nerve. I mumbled something about acting and then offered her a hotel room. She declined and got up and walked away. And I felt awful. She wanted someone to talk to, not a hotel room. I walked home disgusted with my inability to be vulnerable with someone who needed it.

I called my mom and told her what I wished I'd said to that woman, just like I always did when I wished I'd said or done any number of things in the past three years, the past ten years, my whole life.

And my mom said, "Sarah, life is a journey. Every step takes you to the next step you need to go. So spread your wings and fly, because the sky is the limit."

She was at the airport.

Conclusion

THIS IS THE CONCLUSION. I had an introduction so I figured I needed a conclusion. But I don't have one. There is no conclusion. Just like in life. Is that deep? I hope so.

Please don't ask for your money back because there is no conclusion. Actually, you know what, there is a conclusion. You're going to write it. It's not for me to say what you should take away from this book. What kind of anti-authoritarian would I be if I told *you* what to take away from my book? Damn I'm good.

Below, please write down three of your key takeaways from this book. Things that made you laugh, think, cry, feel horny for me, etc.

1.

2.

3.

And there you have it. Please share your conclusions on social media with the hashtag #FoolishConclusions, if hashtags still exist at that time.

Okay, okay, fine, twist my arm. This is what I learned: I learned from George that you can follow all the rules and still be happy and fulfilled. I learned from Charmaine that I want to be loved for what makes me different, not what makes me the same. And I learned from Rachael that I love making people laugh, and I'm more than willing to risk humiliating myself to do it.

Some people say never give up. I say give up! Give up every day. Quit, constantly. Tell yourself you can't take it anymore. Break up with your dreams. Over and over again. And then the next day, give it one more shot. Every day. Quit and then keep trying. Over and over and over again. For the rest of your life.

Like a damn fool.

Thank You

YOU: **THANK YOU FOR WATCHING,** listening, sharing, showing up, and giving me any amount of your attention. You changed my life.

Susan Raihofer: Thank you for being my champion and my partner from day one.

Jill Schwartzman: Thank you for all your ideas and your patience and giving me deadlines or else we both know I'd still be writing this.

Amy Thomasson: Thank you for appearing like an angel from heaven/Canada to help me finish this.

Lance Cooper Sr., Jennifer Cooper, George Cooper, Charmaine Cooper, Rachael Cooper, Susie Cooper, Ryan and Tyler Cooper, Ann-Marie and Aiden Bernstein, Marva Powell: Thank you for your unconditional love and support. And the endless material.

Jamaica. Kingston, Bull Savannah, Runaway Bay, Mandeville, Montego Bay, Negril. Patois. Patties and cocoa bread. Ginger beer.

Jeff Palm and Stella Cooper Palm: Thank you for always making me laugh.

Stacey Kroto, Hilary Smith, Wendy Devaney, Abla Hamilton, Sarah Rankin, Katie Fritts, Brittan Bright, Katie Morrissey, Sari Wong, Polly Rodriguez, Nikki MacCallum, Danna Banana, Alex Porras, Irene McGee: Thank you for your friendship.

Cannon Road Elementary School, White Oak Middle School, Redland Middle School, Colonel Zadok Magruder High School, University of Maryland, College Park, Georgia Institute of Technology, and every online and in-person workshop I've ever taken, which is too many to list here.

Sue Winstead. Mrs. Atanossian. Michael D'Anna. Janet Murray. Shelley Mitchell. Rick Crom. Dan Smith. Nancy Banks. Leigh Wilson Smiley. Joan Rosenberg. Thank you for being brilliant teachers.

Stella Adler Studio of Acting, Upright Citizens Brigade, Laughing Buddha Comedy, Eastville Comedy Club, Comedy Cellar, New York Comedy Club, Broadway Comedy Club, Gotham Comedy Club: Thank you for the stage time.

IQTV, Yahoo!, Flickr, Polyvore, Google, *The Cooper Review*: Thank you to my work families.

Patty Rice, Kirsty Melville, and everyone at Andrews McMeel who made my first books possible.

Michelle Buteau, Sarah Silverman, Amy Schumer, Chelsea Handler, Wanda Sykes, Tiffany Haddish, Quinta Brunson, Issa Rae, Whoopi Goldberg, Tina Fey, Amy Poehler, Mindy Kaling, and every woman who's been funny anywhere, thank you for showing me the way.

Netflix, Natasha Lyonne, Maya Rudolph, Danielle Renfrew Behrens, Paula Pell, Fred Armisen, Chris Burns, and everyone who made and/or watched *Sarah Cooper: Everything's Fine.*

CBS Studios, Nina Tassler, Denise Di Novi, Joan Boorstein, Cindy Chupack, Natalie Morales, Amy Landecker, Josh Charles, Saamer Usmani, Alice Lee, and every single person who worked on our pilot for *How to Be Successful Without Hurting Men's Feelings.*

Ricky Gervais: Thank you for the inspiration and the wisdom.

Jerry Seinfeld, Spike Feresten, Beau Bauman, Cherylanne Martin, Amy Schumer, Adrian Martinez, Jack McBrayer, Melissa McCarthy, Jim Gaffigan, Mikey Day, Bobby Moynihan, Teressa Hill, Rachael Harris, and everyone on the set of *Unfrosted.*

Roundabout Theatre Company, Barry Edelstein, Anna Ziegler, Lucy Freyer, Eddie Kaye Thomas, David Klasko, Katie Holmes: Thank you for teaching me things too big to fit in this book.

Madison Guest, Miguel Lledo: You are magicians.

Allysa Mahler, Mike Berkowitz, Tom Wellington, Kathleen

Lewis, April King, David Kalodner, Marissa Hurwitz, Lewis Kay, and Jared Levine: Thank you for *everything.*

Dina Zuckerberg, Karen Lazarus, Stephanie Paul: Thank you for creating a community that's so desperately needed. Please consider making a donation at myFace.org.

I stand with the Writers Guild of America, the Screen Actors Guild - American Federation of Television and Radio Artists, and unions everywhere.

About the Author

SARAH COOPER lives in Brooklyn with her three adorable plants. They're fake and they're spectacular.

Author photograph by Phil Provencio